W9-AGD-174

TWICE*B*LESSED

TWICE*B*LESSED

*Encouragement for the Caregiver
and Carereceiver*

LAURA Z. SOWERS

BROADMAN
&HOLMAN
PUBLISHERS

Nashville, Tennessee

0-8054-2715-5

Published by Broadman & Holman Publishers
Nashville, Tennessee

Dewey Decimal Classification: 242.4
Subject Heading: TERMINALLY ILL \ DEVOTIONAL
LITERATURE \ CAREGIVERS

Unless otherwise noted, Scripture quotations are from the
Holy Bible, New International Version, copyright © 1973, 1978,
1984 by International Bible Society. Other versions include: NASB,
New American Standard Bible, © the Lockman Foundation, 1960,
1962, 1963, 1968, 1971, 1972, 1973, 1975, 1977; used by per-
mission; TLB, The Living Bible, copyright © Tyndale House
Publishers, Wheaton, Ill., 1971, used by permission; and NKJV,
New King James Version, copyright © 1979, 1980, 1982, Thomas
Nelson, Inc., Publishers.

1 2 3 4 5 6 7 8 10 09 08 07 06 05

Dedication

For Craig

My husband, my best friend, my love

Acknowledgments

Sincere thanks to my editor, Len Goss, and the good people at Broadman & Holman Publishers. When I was diagnosed with leukemia, rather than losing faith in my ability to complete this book, you came alongside with faithful prayers and offers of assistance. Your confidence in this book and concern for me were a great encouragement.

Since dealing with a serious illness, I have a new understanding and appreciation for the strength that comes from the body of Christ. Many thanks to my eternal friends Gena Baker, Karen Funnell, Bill and Susan Conner, Sharon Brundage, Harriet Byrd, and our couples' Bible study. To Terry Ash and the elders and members of Desert Spring Church; you exemplify a church in which Jesus is Lord of all. Old friends Vicky Anderson, Carole Ball, Baker Morrow, JoAnn Strathman, Phil Menicucci, and Paul Harris proved themselves good as gold. A special note of love to my brother, Steve Lawrence.

I would be remiss if I failed to mention my doctors: Dr. Douglas Clark, my oncologist in Albuquerque, New Mexico, and my transplant doctor, Dr. Vinod Pullarkat at City of Hope in Duarte, California. I can't forget Darren, my bone marrow donor who, through his priceless and selfless gift, has given me another chance at life.

Last but not least, I want to thank my family for their unflagging love and support. To my daughter, Cara: Where would I be without your rallying the warriors to prayer at a moment's notice and your wise and tireless input on this book? To my son, Marc: You not only kneeled to pray for me; you stood to keep our business running when Craig was dominated with my care. To my son-in-law, Tim, and my daughter-in-law, Cara Margaret: I could not imagine your being more supportive. You're the best! And then my precious grandchildren, who keep my eyes fixed firmly on the future. I love you Luke, Drew, Ben, Caitlyn, and Cole!

Contents

Introduction

*E*very book has its story, and this one is no exception. In the same month both my parents were diagnosed with cancer. Mom's fifteen-year battle with lymphoma had come back in a more deadly form, and Dad, who was in the mid-stages of Alzheimer's disease, was diagnosed with advanced lung cancer. My parents had been divorced for some forty years, so each of their needs, resources, and attitudes was strongly individual and separate, yet both required one hundred percent of my efforts.

I was making unprecedented decisions for my parents, giving vast amounts of time, and confronting the sad truth of the end of my longest and most basic earthly relationships. Not surprisingly, it was at this time of great demands that my daily times of Bible study and prayer took on a new fervency. Never before had I opened my Bible with greater need or greater expectations. The Lord faithfully guided me through his Word and opened my mind and heart to freshly see that the Bible was divine—speaking to my circumstances with a powerful relevancy. I discovered that the Word of God had something to say to every situation, every tear, every "unsolvable" problem, and every unknown path.

This book is the result of these experiences. It is the book I longed for when my parents and I were at the crossroads of life and death. It is what I found when I searched the Bible looking for ways to help my parents see past their circumstances and look to the light of the Savior and their heavenly home.

My father died on Valentine's Day, and Mother died the following year on Mother's Day. Looking back, I confess that there were times through my parents' illnesses when I honestly yearned for the Lord to take each of them and spare both them and me the trials of illness leading to death. But now I know with certainty that there are lessons that can only be learned by experiencing God's faithful sufficiency through trials and suffering. We not only learn how to care for others in their time of need; we learn about our own vulnerability, the inevitability of death, the importance of a life well lived, and the joyful confidence of an eternity securely fixed. Anything that drives us to the Lord—even heartbreak—has eternal value and rewards.

When I approached my publisher with the idea of a devotional book that ministered both to the caregiver and to the carereceiver, we realized it would be a challenge for one person to address the needs of both groups of readers. Having been a caregiver myself, I could write from my direct perspective and experience, and since my experiences with my parents were so fresh, I believed I could maintain a respectful compassion and insight into the needs of the carereceiver, as well.

But God had a different plan. When I was more than halfway through writing this book, I became sick. After weeks of trying various medicines, my doctor ordered lab work and then called with the shocking news that I had acute myelogenous leukemia. At age fifty-two, after a history of good health, suddenly, I was gravely ill. My formerly independent life became a procession of hospitalizations, chemotherapy treatments, trips to the emergency room, and almost daily contact with doctors and nurses. Where once I was in the driver's seat of caring for others, I was now a passenger being cared for *by* others.

It didn't take long for me to notice something profound: *Imaging* the needs of the carereceiver and *experiencing* those needs are two vastly different things!

Although I achieved remission after half a year of chemo, I relapsed only six months later, exactly a year to the day I was originally diagnosed. Now, my choices narrowed to a dramatic but hopeful option: Bone Marrow Transplant. In his time, God provided the donor and we packed our car and headed to California for what we knew would be a minimum of one hundred days.

The transplant appears to be a success—thank the Lord. The experience, however, redefined my perception of being a "carereceiver" and a child of God. For weeks on end, when I was hospitalized, I was completely without strength and separated by pain and confusion from my normal avenues of faith. My dear Craig was my moment-by-moment lifeline and my connection to supportive family, friends—and to the Lord—a humbling and clarifying illustration of God's power being magnified in the face of utter weakness.

And so it is with gratitude and awe for our Lord that this book has come to be. God patiently granted me his grace, and the result is a book that has been a labor of love, hope, and a chronicle of a personal journey of challenges and growth.

How to Use This Book

The line between the caregiver and the carereceiver may appear to be drawn in indelible ink, but that is an illusion I can attest to. In truth, what separates us is more like the fragile ripples of wind-blown sands. It became clear through caring for my parents and my own illness that the greatest need of the living and the dying is the same—the certainty of salvation. The devotions in this book strive to take the spiritual pulse of the reader and point him or her to the Savior. Peppered throughout the book are devotions that provide the opportunity to make the decision to receive Jesus as Savior and Lord. At the end of the book is a model prayer of salvation should either reader want to make that life-changing choice.

The book is organized in two major sections: Caregiver Devotions and Carereceiver Devotions. You may find your own way of using this book, but I believe there are at least three different approaches.

• **Two Readers, Cover to Cover:** The caregiver and the carereceiver could each choose to read the book from start to finish. Hopefully, the result would be personal comfort and a deeper understanding of each other at this crucial time.

• **Two Readers, Half-and-Half:** The caregiver can mark his place in the caregiver section, and the carereceiver can mark his place in his section, so the devotions can be read individually and at separate paces.

• **Caregiver, Read Aloud to Carereceiver:** Another approach would be for the caregiver to read his or her devotions privately and then read the carereceiver devotions aloud. This could open up communication and reveal spiritual or emotional needs that might otherwise be unspoken.

The last section of the book is called "The Promiser Keeps His Promises"—a special selection of promises and Scriptures of hope, comfort, and encouragement chosen with the needs of caregivers and carereceivers in mind. Each topic is accompanied with a reminder of the character and sufficiency of our Lord.

Some Final Thoughts

In this book I have concentrated on the caregiving and receiving needs of elderly parents and their grown children. While there are millions of baby boomers now caring for their parents, I realize that caregiving and carereceiving may take many forms and countless combinations of diverse relationships.

Regardless of your individual circumstances and the challenges you are facing, my prayer for you is that through your own journey of caregiving or carereceiving, you will look steadily toward Jesus, the Source of care, wisdom, love, and eternal hope.

—Laura Sowers

CAREGIVER DEVOTIONS

The Greatest Care

*"But seek first his kingdom and his righteousness,
and all these things will be given to you as well."*
MATTHEW 6:33

As we left the doctor's office, Dad was oblivious to the grim diagnosis he had just received. Buffered by the fog of the middle stages of Alzheimer's, his only care was to leave the probing doctor and the chilly examining room and return home. The ghostly mass on his chest X-ray drifted from his thoughts the moment it was out of view.

While his cares dissipated, my cares were escalating dramatically. Dad had lung cancer—and in the advanced stages! This news changed everything. His current precarious living situation must now give way to some form of consistent supervised care and my own daily involvement.

The doctor walked us to the elevator. When Dad was out of hearing range, he said softly, "I'll write an authorization for hospice care. The sooner you can get them involved, the better for everyone."

My mind swam with sorrow and worry. There was so much to think about and so many hard decisions yet to make. *What*, I wondered, *do I do first?*

When the crisis of a loved one's illness enters our life, we face a temptation to let these new demanding circumstances become the center of our lives. Jesus knew that there would be times when the cares of this world would threaten to overwhelm our peace of mind and, more importantly, our devotion to him.

Knowing this tendency, Jesus cautioned us about our daily priorities. "But seek first his kingdom," he told us. We may inwardly resist: *"I'd like to spend time with you, Lord, but I have too much to do!"* Precisely why time in the Word and in prayer *must* be given first priority in our day.

As caregivers of any kind—whether physical, emotional, or spiritual—our ability to care for others is dependent on nurturing the *greatest care* of our lives: being rightly related to the Savior. We can't help being shaken by the advent of a serious illness, but if we start our day by seeking God and his will, we can stand in his strength as we care for our loved one.

Heavenly Father,
Guide me through this sad and confusing time.
Enable me to see that the greatest source of strength
for my loved one and for myself will be established
day by day as I seek you and your kingdom. Amen.

Psalm for the Soul

The LORD performs righteous deeds,
And judgments for all who are oppressed.
He made known His ways to Moses,
His acts to the sons of Israel.
The LORD is compassionate and gracious,
Slow to anger and abounding in lovingkindness.
(Ps. 103:6–8 NASB)

Edited Prayers

The men of Israel sampled their provisions
but did not inquire of the LORD.
JOSHUA 9:14

We've all heard that "God helps those who help themselves." Sometimes this phrase is spoken with such conviction, one would think it was Scripture rather than a simple old saying. Clearly, the idea of self-sufficiency is deeply ingrained in our culture. As a result, we may unconsciously edit our prayers by holding back on issues or problems that we believe we can handle on our own. By placing limits on what we pray about, we are inclined to save only the "biggies" for God. For instance, we might pray that a loved one be healed of cancer but decide not to bother God about the stress of our job. We might pray for wisdom and skill for the surgeon who will operate on our parent but fail to ask for the stamina and patience we need to keep up the rigors of caregiving.

Is that what God wants? Does this edited way of relating to him expand our knowledge of him, or does it keep God safely on his turf while we take care of the day-to-day business of life? The problem with this thinking is that we may not realize we have entered into something we can't handle until we have already made decisions and taken actions that will have far-reaching consequences.

In the Old Testament we see Joshua in this situation. As a godly and capable military and spiritual leader of Israel, he was exemplary in seeking God's will and following it with obedience. Yet in at least one instance, Joshua and the Israelites relied on their own perceptions without seeking God's will, and they suffered the consequences.

Word of Joshua's military victories had spread throughout the land. In response, many of the kings in surrounding areas came

TWICE *B*LESSED

together and decided to make war with Israel. The people from Gibeon knew it was just a matter of time before Israel's army wiped them out, so they formulated a plan to trick Joshua into signing a treaty with them. They sent a delegation to meet with Joshua and carefully created an image of weary travelers from far away rather than from neighboring Gibeon. They loaded their donkeys with worn-out sacks and old wineskins and wore patched sandals, ragged clothes, and packed supplies of moldy bread. So when they declared they were from a great distance away and feigned an interest in the God of Israel, Joshua trusted his own ability to assess the situation and didn't consult God before signing a treaty with them. As a result, Israel was not able to eliminate all the peoples living in the land, as God had instructed, and the Gibeonites were cursed with being slaves forevermore.

When we edit our prayers, we deprive God of being Master of all. We inflict unnecessary hardships on ourselves and possibly on others as well. Even when we think the facts are laid out clearly before us, praying for God's guidance can only reap rewards and blessings and spare us untold hardships.

Heavenly Father,
It may take my whole life to really understand
that you want to be Lord of all. Bring to my mind
to consult you about matters I might otherwise
withhold. I may feel foolish and helpless as I do,
but I trust that you will draw me close as I draw
closer to you. In Jesus' name. Amen.

Psalm for the Soul

Glory in his holy name;
let the hearts of those who seek the LORD rejoice.
Look to the LORD and his strength;
seek his face always. (Ps. 105:3–4)

Good Gifts

*"If you then, though you are evil, know how to give good gifts
to your children, how much more will your Father in heaven
give the Holy Spirit to those who ask him!"*

LUKE 11:13

*I*n the first few days following Dad's diagnosis of lung cancer, I walked around in a stunned daze. My husband and
children were great sources of strength and support, but
none of us had a clue about what to do next.

In my prayers I asked God for wisdom and guidance, but the
unspoken cry of my heart was for comfort. I longed for someone
to talk to who had been down the crooked road we faced. My
questions were at once detailed and specific and general and shape-
less. The combination of Dad's problems in view of his inadequate
living situation seemed to be a maddening puzzle with no clear
solution.

On the following Saturday morning, my husband and I went
out to breakfast as we usually did, but at the last minute we chose
a different restaurant. While having our meal, a group of people
passed our table as they were leaving. One of the men looked at
my husband and recognized him as an old friend from high school.
He had moved out of state years ago but was back visiting family.
As he stood at our table, the men hastily tried to catch up on years
apart. We told him the sad news about Dad, and he expressed
his sympathy, then he said good-bye and rushed to catch up with
his group.

A few minutes later, to our surprise, he was back at our table
and asked to join us. He told us that as he was getting into his car,
he felt the Lord was prompting him to come back in and talk more
with us about Dad. He explained that they had been in similar circumstances with his mother. She had recently passed away after a

long struggle with lung cancer and Alzheimer's disease—the very problems Dad had!

As I look back on our conversation, what I remember most clearly is the comfort and reassurance of talking to someone who understood the complexities of what we were facing. Throughout our visit he talked of God's faithful guidance and steady love. What an encouraging message for us to hear at a very discouraging time!

Our Father gives us good gifts. He sees our heart and longs to fill us with his Holy Spirit; he knows our unspoken need and yearns to meet it over and above what we imagine or expect; he feels compassion for his hurting children and delights in comforting them. Whatever the circumstance, he is not baffled, surprised, worried, or confused. He is God.

Dear Father,
You are indeed a good God who gives good gifts.
Thank you for the most precious Gift of all, your
Son, Jesus. Bring to my mind the certainty that there
is no situation too complicated for you. I pray that
I will learn never to withhold asking you for what
I need out of doubt that you are able to do it.
Use this time of trial to multiply my faith and
increase my understanding of who you are.
In Jesus' name. Amen.

Psalm for the Soul

Give thanks to the LORD, for he is good;
his love endures forever (Ps. 107:1)

Seize the Moment

*While Jesus was in Bethany in the home of a man known as
Simon the Leper, a woman came to him with an alabaster
jar of very expensive perfume, which she poured on
his head as he was reclining at the table.*
MATTHEW 26:6–7

There is nothing quite as gratifying as giving the perfect gift at the perfect time. Sometimes our successful gift choice is simply good fortune, but at other times we are so tuned into the situation and needs of another that we are able to respond in just the right way.

In this passage of Scripture, Mary did just that. Jesus had just told his disciples that soon he would be crucified and die. Yet they continued to be dull to what he was saying and misunderstood the imminence of his death. Mary, however, had the spiritual discernment to respond to Jesus. She may not have fully understood the situation, but she knew in her heart that this was the perfect time to show her love and devotion to him with a lavish gesture.

While he reclined at the table, Mary poured precious oil worth three hundred denarii on his head and his feet. Immediately, she was criticized for this extravagant display. Couldn't the money be better used by giving it to the poor? After all, one denarius was a typical day's wages in the Roman world.

Mary had wisely seized the opportunity that would never again exist. She anointed the Lord with oil. In retrospect, this would be the only burial anointing his body would receive, for when the women came to the tomb after his death to care for the body, he was gone.

Cultivating the practice of seizing the moment still requires discernment and the willingness to risk the criticism of others. As we care for our ailing parent or loved one, it's easy to be overwhelmed by the necessary daily responsibilities and overlook a receptive moment that may never again exist. Is this the perfect time to finally share your faith with your dad or mom? Maybe you haven't thanked him or her for all the sacrifices made while you were growing up. Have you taken the risk to plainly say, *"I love you"*? It's not too late now, but one day it will be.

Jesus loved the way Mary sensed the perfect time to show her devotion and her pure worship, and he promised her actions would be long remembered. Don't you suppose that even now our worship and generous devotion resonate in our Lord's heart? Heaven may well be flooded with joy when we seize the moment and pour out our love for him.

Dear Father,
Sometimes I am so dull and slow to recognize
the opportunities you set before me. Wake me up
so that I, like Mary, can bless my loved one by
giving the perfect gift of love at the perfect time.
In Jesus' name. Amen.

Psalm for the Soul
Trust in him at all times, O people;
pour out your hearts to him,
for God is our refuge. (Ps. 62:8)

The Gentle Yoke

"Take my yoke upon you and learn from me. . . . For my
yoke is easy and my burden is light."
MATTHEW 11:29–30

The first time someone referred to me as the caregiver for my dad, I resisted the notion. Inwardly, I denied that he needed a caregiver because he still lived independently and only needed help from me occasionally. I didn't want to feel that I was somehow yoked to him and responsible to care for him throughout the course of his illnesses.

Over time, however, Dad's needs steadily increased and crises ruled the day. Ordinary tasks such as paying his bills had become a backdrop for anger and confusion or outright neglect. He couldn't remember doctor appointments, lunch dates, or phone numbers. He drove erratically and used poor judgment spending money. Occasionally, the situation took a truly frightening turn, like when I got a 2:00 a.m. call from the police telling me they had picked him up when they noticed his aimless and irregular driving. It turned out that he had been driving for hours, unable to find his way home.

Eventually, it was undeniable that Dad needed consistent help to manage safely in the world. His well-being became a concern and a burden that I carried whether I was with him or not. I was indeed yoked to my father, but it was no by means an easy yoke, and the burden was far from light.

These days we rarely think about the imagery and purpose of a yoke. In the context of the times, however, a yoke was used to harness two animals so that they might more efficiently draw their load. To observers, the yoke may have appeared to be a cruel and awkward limitation, but it was, in fact, a blessing to the animals because it enabled them to share their burden and walk in unity.

How interesting that Jesus used the image of a yoke to describe our relationship to him. A yoke suggests hardship, restriction, and burden, so to describe it as easy seems a paradox. Further, Jesus told us to take his yoke willingly—to choose it. In doing so, we reorder our lives by coming in submission to him. Rather than being yoked to our burden, we are joined with the love and might of God who will teach us to walk in unison with his ways. The burden, by default, assumes its rightful place as the load rather than the driving force.

Today you may view yourself as harshly yoked to the person you are caring for rather than kindly yoked to Jesus. If so, I encourage you to set down your clumsy burden and take up the strong and gentle yoke of Jesus. Far from being awkward, constraining, and heavy, his yoke is comfortable—tailor-made for you alone. Let your disciplined walk with him teach the lessons he has for you and calm your anxiety. You are not alone. Jesus is your Partner, bearing your burden and shouldering your cares.

Heavenly Father,
I know that when the work is worthy, you are there
to help me bear it. Thank you for the easy yoke
of your love and strength. Make me strong to trust
your Word and humble to seek your help. Amen.

Psalm for the Soul

"Now I will relieve your shoulder of its burden;
I will free your hands from their heavy tasks."
(Ps. 81:6 TLB)

Posing the Question

For it is with your heart that you believe and are justified, and it is with your mouth that you confess and are saved.
ROMANS 10:10

The diagnosis had been made, and I was told that Dad had only a short time to live. He knew he was experiencing lots of medical tests, but in his dementia he couldn't grasp the big picture. One day, following a visit to the doctor, I drove home the long way through the downtown area and the old country club neighborhood. He was relaxed and happy, and I took the opportunity to ask him an all-important question that I had never asked before.

"Dad," I said, "if you were to die tonight, do you think you would go to heaven?"

He thought for a moment. "Yes," he said simply.

"Why?" I asked.

He chuckled. "Well, certainly not for anything *I've* done."

"Then, why?" I pressed. I didn't know if at this stage of Alzheimer's he would be able to remember or express his beliefs.

"Because of Jesus dying on the cross," he said. A few moments later he added, "I had to repent, you know. I had to ask to be forgiven."

I reached over and squeezed his hand. "And, of course, you were," I said.

What a relief to hear him make the wonderful confession of his beliefs. Dad and I were not really accustomed to discussing spiritual issues, and especially not *personal* spiritual issues. This conversation broke new ground for us and gave me tremendous peace about Dad's future.

On later visits self-consciousness about talking of the Lord seemed to recede. Dad would initiate some interesting spiritual discussions, and more often than not, they were about heaven. "What do you think heaven will be like?" he would say. And together we would ponder the yet-unknown wonders that lay ahead for us. Admittedly, it was easier for me to discuss it knowing that Dad was not aware of the reality hovering over his shoulder. I have wondered if these discussions would have been more awkward if Dad had been fully aware of the imminence of his own death.

In contrast, Mom understood her physical condition, and our conversations were more complex and less comfortable. She didn't seem to enjoy the simple trust in God that Dad had. But we talked about the promises of Jesus that are just as true even when we don't feel a fuzzy, warm glow. We prayed together for peace and reassurance and for trusting her future to her loving God.

If for some reason it seems impossible to discuss these subjects with your parents, hopefully a pastor or close friend can help. This is no time to shy away in avoidance and fear. Wouldn't you pull her back from a cliff if she were about to fall? Posing these difficult questions is one of the priceless opportunities and responsibilities we have to our dying parents.

Heavenly Father,
It's so hard to ask these questions. Yet I love my parents,
and I want the eternal best for them. Help me establish
a dialogue of love that opens the door. Give me courage
to ask the question and wisdom to help them find
the answer: Jesus. Amen.

Psalm for the Soul

But I trust in your unfailing love;
my heart rejoices in your salvation. (Ps. 13:5)

A Chosen Stone

As you come to him, the living Stone—rejected by men but chosen by God and precious to him—you also, like living stones, are being built into a spiritual house to be a holy priesthood, offering spiritual sacrifices acceptable to God through Jesus Christ.

1 PETER 2:4–5

Becoming a caregiver often seems to occur by default. The reasons can be diverse: maybe you are the only child living in the same area as your parent, or perhaps you have siblings, but they are at a different stage in their careers or in raising their own families. Typically, the role of caring for an aging parent falls to the eldest daughter in the family, but maybe you are a daughter-in-law, a niece, or a grandson who finds yourself in the position of caring for a needy relative.

The scenarios are as diverse as families; however, one thing is certain: most caregivers at some point resent the responsibility and the assumption that they will take it. While other family members go about the business and privilege of conducting their own lives and interests, the caregiver squeezes his or her life within the confines of the needs of another. Given the restrictions and constancy of caregiving, it's tempting to feel that circumstances have somehow conspired against us.

In truth, however, when we are submitted children of God, nothing about our lives or our future falls to chance. Through the writing of Peter, God brings an interesting perspective to our function and worth in his kingdom: We are referred to as living stones in his spiritual house. Each person, like each stone of a temple, is carefully chosen and placed to bring strength and beauty to the structure.

As caregivers, we also have been carefully chosen for our unique role. However, we must remember that one stone does not make a temple; other stones are needed. With this in mind, we can feel perfectly confident and justified when we are able to share caregiving responsibilities with other family members.

Following the humbling analogy of being stones, Peter then reminds us that we believers are privileged to become a holy priesthood. Rather than offering animal sacrifices as was required of the priests under the Mosaic Law, we bring spiritual sacrifices that are acceptable and highly valued by God. He looks with favor on acts of worship, praise, good works, the sacrifice of possessions, and the time we give in service. Interestingly, these are the common sacrifices that accompany caregiving. The Lord loves our selfless service, but we must remember that our strength for the task can only endure if we are positioned squarely on the Cornerstone—Jesus Christ.

Heavenly Father,
Sometimes I am angry and frustrated with my
many responsibilities. At other times I feel forgotten
and taken for granted. Remind me of how you regard
this ministry of caregiving and grant me peace and
strength. Give me the courage to ask for help and
participation from other family members and the
grace to accept the outcome. Amen.

Psalm for the Soul

Even the darkness will not be dark to you;
the night will shine like the day
for darkness is as light to you. (Ps. 139:12)

Pray for Me

*I*n just a matter of hours, I had gone from feeling productive and healthy to lying in bed with an escalating fever. Over the next nine days my fever bounced from low-grade to times when it was well over 102 degrees. The doctor said it was a bad, but passing, case of influenza. However, after several more days, the fever continued, so the doctor ordered lab work that brought shocking news: I had leukemia. Within hours I was hospitalized. Suddenly my understanding of the needs of the sick and those receiving care was dramatically broadened.

When we are healthy and strong, it's difficult to understand the true needs of the sick. Looking at the limitations of illness through the lens of vibrant health tends to impair our ability to empathize. But during my illness I saw what a profound effect pain and suffering have on one's ability to draw on faith. My normal avenues to connecting with my faith suddenly fell short. I couldn't comfortably read the Word; I had little interest in listening to radio programs; and I lacked the strength to talk on the phone with believing friends. When I mentally searched for those comforting promises from Scripture, I could recall only fragments. I struggled to formulate prayers, but they were reduced to the most elementary form.

One of the most valuable and comforting things my husband did for me while I was sick was to pray aloud for me. As I listened, I attached myself to his prayers and let his voice serve as my own. As he talked to God on my behalf, he also reconnected me to my faith that had dimmed in the atmosphere of pain. His prayers and affirmations of God's love reminded me that God was not indifferent to my suffering although he seemed silent and far away.

Even if the one you are caring for has walked with the Lord through decades of life and trials, now may be a time when he or she desperately needs you to come alongside with the offering of verbal prayers, reading from the Word, and reminders of the promises reserved for believers.

The apostle Paul prayed diligently for the church and freely asked—no—begged for prayer for himself and his ministry. Our prayers for one another are not only tokens of our love; they hold enormous potential. The value of the prayers of a righteous person cannot be estimated. Our prayers bolster the faith of those who are weak and allow us the great privilege of partaking in the blessings that our prayers will bring.

Lord God,
One of the joys of being a believer is lifting those we
love to you in prayer. Let me be quick to offer verbal prayer,
reading from the Word, and remembering aloud your
promises. Right now I don't fully understand the needs,
fears, and limitations that illness can bring. But I under-
stand the power of your Word and your love. Make me
sensitive and bold to be the voice of faith for my
loved one. In Jesus' name. Amen.

Psalm for the Soul

May my prayer come before you;
turn your ear to my cry. (Ps. 88:2)

Honor-Bound

"Honor your father and mother."
MATTHEW 15:3

When we are children, it's clear that God wants us to honor our parents by being obedient and conforming to the disciplines of life that they teach us. When we do, we not only show respect for their wishes; we also greatly increase the probability of functioning well in the world and avoiding many of the dangers that can cut life short. The disciplines cultivated in childhood make us useful contributors to society, and, best of all, living a long life gives us more opportunity to grow in our relationship to the Lord. The benefits of honoring our parents when we are kids are clear, but as adults, how do we honor our parents in their old age? Do we really have a biblical obligation to them?

For centuries people have tried to wiggle out of the responsibility of caring for their parents. The Pharisees were particularly sly and creative about it. They had a convenient provision that they believed superseded the law and wisdom of God. If a person made a gift to the priests of his or her worldly possessions rather than directing those resources toward caring for their elderly parents, they were released from the responsibility of caring for them (vv. 5–6). I'm sure for some, this was a way of killing two birds with one stone; they were able to look spiritual and pious while simultaneously avoiding the obligation of caring for their folks. This certainly served the financial interests of the Pharisees and provided a sanctified escape hatch for those who wanted to evade the duty of caring for elderly parents.

Jesus, of course, saw right to the heart of this setup and called it just what it was: hypocrisy. He condemned the practice of giving to God when it interfered with the responsibility of caring for parents; it was in direct contradiction to the teachings of Jesus and the fifth commandment to honor one's parents. It also slandered the character of God, suggesting he would want that which should belong to the parents.

Unfortunately, in our twenty-first-century culture, the whole concept of honor is growing dim. We might even go to the other extreme and tend to exaggerate the meaning, but honor doesn't mean placing an individual on a pedestal and ordering life around him; rather, it is an appropriate respect that shows itself in speaking kindly and thinking and doing well for another.

The godly application of honoring parents certainly includes caring for their needs when they are in the distress of old age. Regardless of whether our parents are sweet or cranky, rich or poor, sick or well, believers or unbelievers, the teaching is clear: we are to honor them.

Dear Lord,
At the most painful, demanding, and selfless point
of your ministry on the earth—the cross—you made
sure that the future needs of your mother would
be met. You entrusted her care to your beloved disciple
who took Mary into his home that very day. Help me
care for my parents in a way that pleases you. Lord,
you know this isn't easy because of the nature and
complexities of the relationship with my parents.
Therefore, let my love and reverence for you
be evident in the way I care for them. Amen.

Psalm for the Soul

I remember your ancient laws, O LORD,
and I find comfort in them. (Ps. 119:52)

Following His Footprints

Jesus' disciples asked him, "Where do you want us to go and
make preparations for you to eat the Passover?" . . .
"Go into the city, and a man carrying a jar of water
will meet you. Follow him."
MARK 14:12–13

During the course of each of my parents' illnesses, there came a time when they could no longer manage in their own homes. Dad's needs were especially challenging because in addition to lung cancer, his Alzheimer's disease affected his judgment and made supervision a necessity.

Unfortunately, Dad was not able to understand the needs of his illnesses, and he hotly resisted any change. Taking all these factors into consideration, I approached the task of making arrangements for him with apprehension.

The disciples faced a different challenge when making arrangements for the Passover Feast they would share with Jesus. This sacred festival of Judaism was an important event, and they wanted the plans to please their Teacher. Wisely, their first step was to ask Jesus for guidance, which he gave in detail. Two disciples were to go to the city and look for a man carrying a jar of water. In those times it was usually the women who carried the water, so this was out of the ordinary. Once they found the man, he would lead them to the owner of the house where the room and its furnishings would be ready for the Lord and his disciples to eat the Passover Feast.

How I would have loved to have Jesus direct me in such detail! It would have been wonderful if he'd said to me, "Look for a man carrying a water pot" (or a coffeepot, or a flowerpot!), "and when you find him, follow him home, and that's where you should move your father."

Through much more normal means, the Lord did lead, and the difficult move was made. But despite being in a pleasant setting, Dad never adjusted to his environment. This sad fact brought me many times of doubt and self-recrimination. It made me review my decision-making and remind myself that I had followed the Lord's footprints as closely as I could in the shifting sands of Dad's illnesses. Finally, and most important, I came to the point of accepting the fact that my earthly father would never be pleased with his circumstances, so I had to rely instead on pleasing my heavenly Father.

As caregivers for our parents, we are often called upon to make unprecedented decisions on their behalf. The weight and fear that accompany these decisions can feel overwhelming. Yet we are not alone. Just as with his disciples, the Lord delights in being a part of our planning, and he still goes quietly before us to prepare the way.

Look for his footprints not in the sand but in his Word, through answered prayers, through the godly counsel of other believers, and through discernment as you take practical steps.

Heavenly Father,
There are times when I yearn for a sign from you that will
confirm the hard decisions I am making. Let me look for
you where you have promised to be found—in your
Word. Speak to me so clearly that I cannot misunderstand.
Like the Sovereign Ruler who went before the disciples,
go before me. I pray that I will follow you
so closely, I cannot get lost. Amen.

Psalm for the Soul

Righteousness will go before Him,
And shall make His footsteps our pathway. (Ps. 85:13 NKJV)

A Talent for Giving

"Well done, good and faithful servant! You have been faithful
with a few things; I will put you in charge of many things.
Come and share your master's happiness!"
MATTHEW 25:21

The parable of the talents is rich with meaning and lessons. Each of three servants was entrusted with talents (money) by their master. They were given varying amounts that corresponded to their abilities. The master expected them to seize their opportunity and to improve upon their gift in some way. Two of the three did exactly that, but the third, entrusted with the least money, fearfully hid it in a hole. He then justified his laziness and lack of enterprise on the grounds that his master was a hard man with high expectations.

I believe that the opportunities and challenges of caregiving are comparable to the responsibility faced by the servants caring for their master's talents. It may seem strange to regard the solemn role of caregiving as a gift, but often it is through the process of behaving responsibly that the gift is realized. Further, when we make the mental leap from looking at caregiving as haphazardly foisted upon us rather than carefully entrusted to us by our Lord, we have taken a giant step forward.

Most people would readily agree that Mother Teresa had a remarkable talent for giving to the sick and the dying. But even her ministry began with her obedience to respond to God-ordained circumstances: One day Mother Teresa came upon a dying woman in the street. She had been half eaten by rats and ants. Rather than turning away from this appalling sight, she took the dying woman to the hospital and refused to leave until she had received care. Mother Teresa then noticed that there were other people dying in the streets of Calcutta, so she went to the town hall and asked for a place to take these destitute individuals. She was directed to a vacant building and, within hours, The Home for the Dying was started.

Mother Teresa said that her mission was not one of social work; she wanted only to bring the joy and peace of Jesus to the people. God richly honored her faithful response to the opportunity he placed before her in the street that day.

Most of us are not drawn to the hard task of caring for the sick and dying. But even if we are responding with difficulty and out of dutiful responsibility, we can be certain that God is at the heart of it, and he is pleased with our faithfulness.

> Lord God,
> I am not a paragon of selfless virtue as Mother Teresa
> seemed to be. My duties of caring for someone who is
> ill and dying challenge me and drive me to you and
> your Word out of sheer weakness and need. I pray that
> you will honor my efforts, and let me bring your love
> and your joy to the one I care for. Thank you for
> entrusting this opportunity to me. Give me your
> strength to do it justice. Amen.

Psalm for the Soul

For the LORD loves the just
and will not forsake his faithful ones. (Ps. 37:28)

God-Confidence

Dear friends, if our hearts do not condemn us, we have confi-
dence before God and receive from him anything we ask,
because we obey his commands and do what pleases him. And
this is his command: to believe in the name of his Son, Jesus
Christ, and to love one another as he commanded us.

1 JOHN 3:21–23

After weeks of prayer, consulting with Dad's doctors, and researching the options, I moved Dad to a group home. I had looked at many different homes that weren't right for one reason or another, so when I found a nice one that fit his needs and was close to me, I took it as an answer to prayer. I talked it over with the family, but unfortunately I wasn't able to consult with Dad. He had become resistant to any kind of change and couldn't grasp the complexities and dangers of his health problems.

After the move, I tried to help him adjust. We took walks, read books, and just spent time together. But the moment I left, he was unhappy and restless. Even when I was away from him, his well-being dominated my thoughts. When an elderly family member changed from being supportive to attacking my decisions, I felt defeated. Mentally I reviewed my actions. Hadn't I prayed about this? I thought I had made the best decision in view of the circumstances, but was I hasty? Should I have waited for a dramatic sign from heaven? Had I really followed God's leading?

If you're fortunate, your parent will be aware when his needs and limitations necessitate a change. If not, as you make prayerful decisions for him, you may find that you're met with resistance, criticism, or judgments from others. There may be no happy resolution that wins the approval of everyone. In fact, this may be a time when you have to move forward in unprecedented reliance on God and wean yourself of the need to please other people.

Certainly, as John says in this passage, we need to look inward and see if our heart is condemning us. If it isn't, we must trust and be confident that God is working through the present circumstances and guiding our decisions. It's easy to become overly focused on our own actions and motives until we obscure our focus on the Lord and the real issues: Are we walking with him daily, hourly, moment-by-moment? Are there areas of sin that we've not confessed? If so, we must confess them at once so that we can pray in confidence before God and keep the way clear for his faithful response.

Following God's will does not guarantee an easy path. The hard truth is that Dad never came to the point where he liked and accepted where he was. But it became clear day by day that it was the right decision—even if it was not an easy one.

Lord,
Prayer takes on a new dimension when it must be
followed with decisive actions for my parent. I know
the key to answered prayer is abiding in you. Help me
understand that abiding means continuing in you,
remaining in you, standing in you, and enduring
in you. Let my love for you take the form of clear
obedience and quick confession when I sin.
In Jesus' name. Amen.

Psalm for the Soul

Create in me a pure heart, O God,
and renew a steadfast spirit within me. (Ps. 51:10)

Friendly Fire

"You intended to harm me, but God intended it for good."
GENESIS 50:20

*I*t is estimated that 21 percent of the wounded and casualties in World War II were the result of friendly fire. In the confusion of battle, our own soldiers mistakenly fired on their own rather than the enemy—a tragic situation for both parties.

In the Bible, Joseph experienced an intentional form of friendly fire when his jealous brothers sold him into slavery. In spite of his trust in them, they turned their fears and ambitions against him, only stopping short of killing him. They returned home to their father bearing Joseph's distinctive coat dipped in animal blood to validate their story of his death.

In a contemporary application, nothing is quite as upsetting as coming under verbal fire and criticism from someone we trusted and thought was on our side. I know this firsthand. When Dad had reached the point in his illnesses when he required constant care in a safer environment, his elderly sister, who had a long history of instability, became enraged at my decisions. Despite my efforts to include her, enlist her support, and help her make the difficult adjustment, she began what could only be called a campaign of assault. She waged her war with lengthy hate-filled letters, venomous phone calls, messages left on my answering machine, and the enlistment of people I'd never met who called and offered their criticisms.

This fell outside the realm of all the expected sorrows that accompany the illness and death of a parent. I felt completely unprepared to defend myself in battle with a relative while simultaneously struggling with the realities of Dad's impending death.

Satan, however, is no respecter of a person who is already stressed to the max when he decides to turn up the heat a little bit. The harsh criticism took a toll on me in that it drove me to excessive self-examination and depression. But it also had a very positive effect because it sent me running to my Lord for comfort, guidance, and wisdom. I prayed constantly that God would calm my troubled relative and bring her to a peace about the situation, but that was not to be.

Joseph's story would not be complete without recognizing that despite the evil intent of his brothers, God's plans were not thwarted. Through a chain of events, Joseph came to Pharaoh's attention and was put in charge of the whole land of Egypt. When the opportunity for payback presented itself, Joseph not only forgave his brothers; he provided for them and their children through years of famine.

Father in Heaven,
The attack from someone I love and trusted hurts so much.
Joseph's faith and reliance on you kept him from becoming
unforgiving and bitter. He blessed those who cursed him,
and in turn, you richly blessed Joseph. Give me a heart
of forgiveness, and let my reliance on you be the constant
in an ever-changing life. In Jesus' name. Amen.

Psalm for the Soul
Turn from evil and do good;
seek peace and pursue it. (Ps. 34:14)

Your Witness

*Therefore, since we are surrounded by such a great cloud
of witnesses, let us throw off everything that hinders and
the sin that so easily entangles, and let us run with
perseverance the race marked out for us.*
HEBREWS 12:1

*I*n our twenty-first-century culture, we are inclined to limit
our understanding of the word *witness* to situations that
occur in the courtroom. In that setting an individual takes
the stand and recalls incidents or individuals he has observed firsthand in a given situation. What that witness says is judged in the
light of his personal integrity and credibility.

In contrast to the common courtroom application, we are
rarely conscious of the daily witness of our lives. Our behavior and
attitudes are constantly being observed, scrutinized, and *witnessed*
by others. Regardless of whether we are dealing with a waitress,
our elderly parent, a bank clerk, or the president of a Fortune 500
corporation, our conduct constitutes the "hard evidence" of our
beliefs that either establishes or erodes our credibility as ones who
live by faith in Jesus.

Chapter 11 of Hebrews is often referred to as the Faith
Chapter. Under the inspiration of the Holy Spirit, the writer of this
book enumerates those Old Testament men and women who held
fast to their faith despite great trials and suffering.

Through the likes of Abel, Abraham and Sarah, Enoch, Noah,
and others, we are able to witness faith in action. Even though
circumstances brought them to the end of their own reasoning,
understanding, abilities, and pride, they trusted God and obeyed
his Word. Because their faith was proven true under pressure, they
have become our role models—even thousands of years later.

Isn't it humbling to realize that our own actions are also being
recorded by those who witness our lives? Our children, regardless

of their ages, never cease observing and learning from our example. And I suspect we would be shocked to grasp the impact of our behavior on the wider community of our acquaintances.

As we prepare to help our parents at the end of their lives, we can be sure that others are taking note of how we—believers in Jesus Christ—are dealing with this challenge. This is difficult stuff, and everyone knows it. They may not say a word, but they will watch to see if it really makes a difference to be a Christian when it comes to the nitty-gritty problems and pressures of life. Can we keep our cool when added responsibilities turn up the heat in our life? Are we kind even when confronted with anger and unreasonableness? Do we show respect and honor long after they can be demanded?

This is our witness, and people are watching.

Dear Lord,
I feel the pressure to be a good witness of my beliefs.
Help me throw off the obstacles that hinder me from
rising to this challenge, like my own personal sin that
rebels at obedience. I know I can't manage this challenge
on my own, so give me strength to stay close to you
as I pray, read your Word, and learn more about
you—the Great Witness of love and compassion.
In Jesus' name. Amen.

Psalm for the Soul

He guides the humble in what is right
and teaches them his way. (Ps. 25:9)

Suffering's Rewards

*In this you greatly rejoice, though now for a little while
you may have had to suffer grief in all kinds of trials.*
1 PETER 1:6

6:10 a.m.: The abrupt ringing of the telephone seemed to resonate in my bones. I checked the caller ID: Dad—again. "I want you to come take me home right now!" he said. The day was beginning just as it had ended the night before, with Dad's confused and constant phone calls.

"I'll be there soon, Dad. We'll talk and have a nice, long visit."

A deep weariness settled over me as I hung up the phone. I scarcely recognized my own life anymore. Dad's emotional needs, persistent confusion, rapidly failing health, and his struggle to adjust to the group home dominated everything. *Someday, this trial will be over, but when, Lord?* The thought was followed by a wave of sadness and guilt, for how could I look forward to the end of this trial without facing the loss it would bring?

One of the great challenges of caring for a loved one through his or her final illness comes from not knowing the duration of the trial. Will it be months? Years? We may feel ashamed of our selfish concerns, but we shouldn't. Caring for someone we love at this crucial time is a shared suffering for both the ill and the one who cares for him.

We have a tendency to regard all suffering as bad, so our first response to a trial is usually to try to find the end to it. The Lord, however, not only allows difficult circumstances; he cherishes them as vulnerable and teachable times in our life. He knows that in the grand scheme of things, our suffering will last only "for a little while," though the rewards can be rich and long lasting.

To be able to see this ourselves, we must cultivate an eternal perspective and search for the blessings and rewards that distinguish

themselves in the midst of suffering. For it is when we are confronted with fading health and the certainty of physical death that
we are most inclined to rejoice in the new birth and living hope
given us through the resurrection of Jesus Christ. Similarly, when we
observe how worldly fortunes can fade with a pessimistic word
from Wall Street, it is then that the imperishable inheritance that
waits for us in heaven is brilliant in its steadfast promise. This life is
fleeting and fraught with pain, but a joyful eternity awaits those
who love and follow the Lord.

Pondering God's gifts and promises as we are going through
trials has the effect of shoring up our feeble faith. Eventually we
will find that, though severely tested, our faith hasn't shattered
at all but has emerged stronger, more genuine, polished by wear
and tears, and has become a quiet praise to the awesome God it
honors.

Heavenly Father,
Help me look past my troubles and be sharply focused
on your eternal plan. Let me bring this perspective
into the daily rigors of caring for the person I love.
Thank you for the blessings that come out of hardship.
Make this a fertile, fruitful time that produces the
qualities you are seeking to cultivate in me. Amen.

Psalm for the Soul

May the LORD answer you when you are in distress;
may the name of the God of Jacob protect you. (Ps. 20:1)

The Hole-in-the-Roof Gang

When they could not find a way to do this because of the crowd,
they went up on the roof and lowered him on his mat through
the tiles into the middle of the crowd, right in front of Jesus.
LUKE 5:19

*I*t must have been a touching scene: Four men carrying their
paralytic friend on a pallet to see Jesus. They had heard
stories of this miracle worker. Hadn't he recently touched a
man suffering with leprosy and cured him? If they could just bring
their beloved friend to Jesus, surely he would heal him too.

When they got to the house where Jesus was, they were met
with an unexpected obstacle. A crowd had gathered and was overflowing out the door. The sight must have crushed their high hopes.
No doubt, they were exhausted from their walk and carrying their
crippled friend. Maybe for a moment they considered abandoning
their plan and heading home, but that thought quickly faded.
Instead, an unusual idea emerged. Carefully, they maneuvered the
pallet up the stairs to the roof of the house.

Now what? Maybe they could hear Jesus' voice in conversation just below them. Imagine their frustration—so near and yet so
far. We don't know whether it was only one man or all four who
knelt and began removing the tiles and digging a hole through the
roof. Eventually, however, they were able to lower their friend into
the room and in front of Jesus.

It must have astonished them when they realized that they had
succeeded. Their friend was finally before the Lord. And then Jesus
spoke: "Friend," he told the paralytic, "your sins are forgiven
you."

Did the four men silently cry: *His sins? What about his legs?*

Jesus saw past the obvious to the greater need of the paralytic. Useless legs would cripple him in life, but unforgiven sins would cripple him for eternity.

The Pharisees were already in a huddle; they viewed Jesus' statement as blasphemy. *Who can forgive sin except God?* they reasoned.

Jesus then healed the man's legs as well, not only out of compassion for the paralytic but also so that the Pharisees would have visible evidence that the man's sins had been forgiven.

What a glorious response to faith!

It's tempting to feel helpless when someone we love is sick and suffering. But if we follow the example of the four men who wouldn't give up on getting their friend to Jesus, we will be on the right path. Although we can't carry our loved one on a pallet and set him before the Savior, we can certainly lift him up in prayer and ask the Lord to heal him—body and soul.

Holy Father,
Let my faith in you make me bold and creative in my
efforts to bring my loved one before you. Give my faith
a voice to talk about your love. Give it feet to serve
as I'm needed. Give it arms to lift up the sick in prayer,
and give it wings to reach your ear. Amen.

Psalm for the Soul

As for me, I said, "O LORD, be gracious to me;
Heal my soul, for I have sinned against You." (Ps. 41:4 NASB)

Commanded to Courage

"Have I not commanded you? Be strong and courageous.
Do not be terrified; do not be discouraged, for the LORD
your God will be with you wherever you go."
JOSHUA 1:9

As the new leader of Israel, Joshua was called to fill big shoes—the shoes of Moses. No matter how willing he was and how much he loved and trusted God, it must have been a daunting prospect. Joshua had the assurance of knowing God was with him just as he had been with Moses, yet over and over, the Lord urged him to be strong and courageous and obedient. In this way God assured Joshua he would meet with success.

Joshua was a military leader, a role in which one would expect to meet with frightening circumstances that would require strength and courage. Yet the Lord reminded him to consciously cultivate these qualities and to aim himself toward those standards. In the atmosphere of faith, the Israelites would be watching him and gauging their behavior to his. By maintaining an attitude of strength and courage, fear would not have opportunity to take root and sprout into deadly doubt.

We may not be leading the Israelites across the Jordan River into the promised land, but in our leadership roles as caregivers, we face our own peculiar challenges. It took me a while to come to grips with this. I tried to convince myself that somehow my parents and I would escape the tougher challenges that come with aging and illness. But that was not to be. Eventually, it was clear that each of my parents needed my help and care. I struggled to understand their limitations and adapt and define my new role. Once I had accepted the responsibility, I was surprised to discover that caring for my parents would at times be frightening and require such courage.

If that seems dramatic, what else but courage is needed when a doctor grimly pronounces the sentence of a deadly disease on your loved one? You realize at once that you are dealing with an unknown and formidable adversary. Then, when the regimen of treatments begins, it can seem almost as overwhelming as the illness. If the disease progresses, great courage will be needed when it becomes clear that changes must take place and difficult decisions are at hand. Will your parent be able to stay alone at home, or is it necessary to bring in help? Will he or she live with you or go into a care facility? On and on, every issue is laden with sorrow, concern, and often with guilt.

Finally, courage must link hands with hope when the time has come to sit at your parent's bedside when the fight is drawing to an end. You will need strength of heart to steadily comfort your weakening parent. You will need courage to pray confidently when the unknown bears down; you will need trust that in spite of this totally foreign terrain, God knows the way and holds your parent—and you—in the grip of his love and grace.

As caregivers we may be more like Joshua than we know. We are stepping in to lead our parents through a tough journey that we pray will culminate in their safe arrival to the promised land.

Dear Father,
You have had to awaken me to these new and strange
responsibilities. In theory I understand, but when it
comes time to take action, I am frightened of the
shifting roles between my parent and me. Help me find my
strength in you and my courage in your unfailing love. Amen.

Psalm for the Soul
Be strong and take heart,
all you who hope in the LORD. (Ps. 31:24)

Comfort-able Friends

*"A despairing man should have
the devotion of his friends."*
JOB 6:14

*J*ob has the distinction of being remembered as one of the
most afflicted men in the Bible. Through a procession of cat-
aclysmic events, Job had lost his children, his servants, his
possessions, and his health. From living at the height of blessing
and protection by the hand of God to the depths of loss and
despair, his suffering and losses were stunning.

It's safe to say that Job's friends were a mixed blessing. Initially,
they came to his side and did nothing but sit with him day and
night for seven days. They were utterly silenced by his dire situation and could only express their caring and sympathy by their
physical presence. They might have done well to leave it at that.
Instead, they embarked on a prolonged discussion about the per-
ceived failings and shortcomings in Job's life that might have
prompted God to allow such great affliction.

Job needed friends, but his friends lacked compassion and
mercy for Job and, most importantly, an understanding of God's
character. Their fundamental beliefs about God ultimately defined
their abilities to comfort and counsel their friend.

Today these same factors still determine our ability to comfort
others. During my parents' illnesses, I could tell within a few minutes of conversation whether a friend really grasped what we were
going through. The caring and prayers of those who understood
often made the difference in my day. There were times when the
thoughtfulness of a friend shone in brilliant contrast to the shadow
of my grief, like the night we came home to a beautifully prepared
home-cooked meal after several days spent going back and forth to
the hospital and managing with fast food. It felt like a hug from
above.

Another friend had the ability to grasp the situation so thoroughly that when she prayed with me, she would sometimes articulate needs that I hadn't even spoken. But not all my friendships fared so well. The rigors and sadness of attending a parent dying of cancer also repelled some people and kept them remote and detached.

Although Job's friends genuinely cared for him and passionately argued the possible causes of his suffering, they missed it all the way around. They lacked the perspective and confidence of knowing that God had a purpose and had defined the perimeters of Job's testing.

Likewise, we may never know or understand the reasons for our suffering. God may be allowing our trials for the purpose of maturing us, deepening our trust in him, and teaching us that the only perfect comforter is God.

Dear God,
Thank you for friends who know and trust you even when
circumstances seem out of control. Let me learn from them
and from my experience as a caregiver so that someday
I might be able to comfort others with the overflowing
comfort I have received from you. Amen.

Psalm for the Soul

My comfort in my suffering is this:
Your promise preserves my life. (Ps. 119:50)

Enduring Joy

Rejoice in the Lord always.
I will say it again: Rejoice!
PHILIPPIANS 4:4

My husband and I sidestepped into the vacant seats of the pew. I shrugged off my coat and tried to shrug off my cares. It had been a dreadful week. A biopsy on a suspicious lump confirmed that Mom's cancer was back in a much deadlier form, and Dad's dementia had kept me running from my home to his. I felt about as joyless as I could remember.

The music started, and I read the words on the screen. My mind looked for comfort, but it felt remote—out of reach. We were well into the second chorus when at last, my heart heard the words: *My Jesus, my Savior, Lord there is none like you!* Something in my spirit quickened. Yes! That was how I felt. The Lord is not some impersonal God; he is *my* Jesus, *my* Savior.

The song continued: *My comfort, my shelter. Tower of refuge and strength.* This week he had been just that to me, the only place I had felt safe from the storm of trouble and the source of the strength that enabled me to be there and be strong for my folks.

Power and majesty, praise to the King! Mountains bow down and the seas will roar at the sound of your name! This Lord of mine is a powerful God. He created the strongest forces of nature, and they stand ready to do his bidding and shout their praise.

I sing for joy at the work of your hands, forever I'll love you, forever I'll stand. Nothing compares to the promise I have in you! This is my enduring joy! It is in the changeless Jesus—the One who is the same yesterday, today, and forever. My joy is in his promises that will never be broken or retracted. He will never leave or forsake me; he will be with me always; he has a plan and a purpose for my life and for my parents' lives. This joy is not dependent on fickle circumstances.

Maybe when Paul issued the command to rejoice to the believers in Philippi, they too were going through trying times. Maybe they stared at him with a you've-got-to-be-kidding look when he told them, "Rejoice in the Lord always." And Paul, sensing their doubt and disbelief, decided to clarify his statement: "I will say it again: Rejoice!"

Lord God,
My faith is being tested in ways I never imagined as
I deal with the realities and complexities of my ailing
parents. But it is partially because of this trial that
I have experienced the unshakable joy of finding
you there in the eye of the storm—calm, loving,
strong, undisturbed by circumstances. In that, in
you, I rejoice. In Jesus' name. Amen.

Psalm for the Soul

My soul will boast in the LORD;
let the afflicted hear and rejoice.
Glorify the LORD with me;
let us exalt his name together. (Ps. 34:2–3)

Thorny Issues

"The one who received the seed that fell among the thorns is the man who hears the word, but the worries of this life and the deceitfulness of wealth choke it, making it unfruitful."
MATTHEW 13:22

Jesus told this portion of the parable of the sower to illustrate the person who had made only a superficial commitment to Christ. At first the individual received God's Word, but being poorly rooted, he fell prey to the distractions of worries and money and abandoned his interest in the Lord.

Even a devoted believer planted in "good soil" needs to be mindful of the antagonistic devices of the devil. Satan knows that at times of sorrow and crisis, we are particularly vulnerable to attack. The many thorny issues and concerns of caregiving make us ripe for neglecting spiritual matters and effectively choking Jesus out of our life.

I learned about the literal kind of thorny weeds when I made my first attempt to grow a garden. I turned over a broad strip of dirt, poked some seeds in the ground, and watered them daily. When my gardener friend came for a visit, I proudly showed her my flower bed, which had sprouted a crew cut of tiny green shoots. She stooped to take a better look and said gently, "I hate to tell you that most of these little guys are weeds. You need to get rid of them, or they'll eventually squeeze out your flowers." Despite my good intentions, I had been nurturing the weeds while compromising the flowers because I had not yet developed the discernment to tell the difference.

Generally our lives are already busy when it becomes necessary to care for a parent or loved one. Then, like weeds counterfeiting as flowers, we allow our many roles and responsibilities to distract us from the quiet but crucial practices of prayer, meditation, and worship.

We may argue that we can't just abandon our duties. Certainly not, but neither can we mindlessly cooperate with Satan's plan to render us ineffective. Consider the devil's perspective: He knows that when we received Christ as Savior, the matter of our eternity was sealed forever. But, if he can't touch our soul, he will gladly settle for keeping us so frantically busy that we neglect our walk with the Lord and become fruitless.

The repercussions are far-reaching. If we have abandoned the Source of our own well-being and strength, how long until we are exhausted, depressed, and unable to maintain our responsibilities or recognize a spiritual opportunity when it arises with our perishing loved one? By being absorbed with regular life compounded with the good work of caregiving, we are distracted from the best opportunity to be effective men and women of God.

Do you see Satan's strategy? It is shrewd, it is subtle, but more than that, it is war.

> *Heavenly Father,*
> *Discernment is never so difficult as when I try to sort*
> *the good thing from the best thing. The best thing is*
> *to walk shoulder to shoulder with you through all my*
> *life and especially during times of stress, sadness,*
> *and worry. Enable me to make the changes that will*
> *honor you and allow for my ongoing growth in the Word.*
> *In Jesus' name. Amen.*

Psalm for the Soul

The righteous will flourish like a palm tree. . . .
They will flourish in the courts of our God.
They will still bear fruit in old age. (Ps. 92:12–14)

Giving What We Have Received

Jesus told this parable: "Two men went up to the temple to pray, one a Pharisee and the other a tax collector. The Pharisee stood up and prayed about himself: 'God, I thank you that I am not like other men—robbers, evildoers, adulterers—or even like this tax collector. I fast twice a week and give a tenth of all I get.'"
LUKE 18:9–11

*M*y conversation with an elderly family member had taken an unusual turn to spiritual matters. Although it was generally an off-limits subject, I took the opportunity to talk about God's saving grace and mercy. She listened politely but squirmed in her chair. "My daddy was a preacher," she said, "and I never heard him say that God loved me. All he ever told me was that at the rate I was going, I was on my way to hell. If it's really true that God loves me no matter what I've done, why didn't my daddy ever tell me so?"

How very sad! While no one but God knows the condition of another's heart, I suspect that her father couldn't pass on God's love and mercy because he had not received them himself. When all we have is a church affiliation and a head full of knowledge, we are ripe to do damage—like carrying a loaded spiritual gun.

Caring for an ailing parent or another loved one provides a prime opportunity to discuss spiritual matters. So often these talks tend to gravitate to "religion," church membership, or good works. But as believers, we can seek the higher ground of avoiding controversy and, instead, continually bringing Jesus front and center.

God was merely a superficial interest of the Pharisee in this parable. What really pleased him was talking about his own righteousness and the credit he deserved for his good works. He pretended to thank God, but it was a thinly veiled opportunity to pat himself on the back for being "right." One wonders why he needed God at all when he clearly felt he could enter heaven on his own merit.

At the other end of the spectrum is the individual who, like the humble tax collector, looks back on his life and realizes he has made one mistake after another. As he stands at the doorway between life and death, he may be filled with regret and fear. Now is a golden opportunity to offer him what you yourself have received. Tell him about Jesus, about his love, his purpose for coming to earth, and the meaning of his death on the cross. He may wonder if he will be reviled if he approaches God at this late date, but humility and repentance touch God's heart now just as they did with the tax collector. God was indeed merciful to him and sent him on his way washed clean of his sins.

It is an awesome joy privilege, and responsibility to share the truth of Jesus and his saving grace. If you search your heart and discover that you can't give it because you have not yet received it, ask God to be Lord of your life and he will make his home with you from this instant on.

Lord God,
Give me courage to tell my loved one about the love
and hope I have in you. I fear being rejected, but
I don't want to hesitate to pass on what I so
eagerly received for myself. Clear away the obstacles
of church affiliation and good works so that nothing stands
before us but you and your love. In Jesus' name. Amen.

Psalm for the Soul

Remember, O LORD, your great mercy and love,
for they are from of old.
Remember not the sins of my youth
and my rebellious ways;
according to your love remember me.
for you are good, O LORD. (Ps. 25:6–7)

Resting Faith

*The night before Herod was to bring him to trial, Peter was
sleeping between two soldiers, bound with two chains,
and sentries stood guard at the entrance.*
ACTS 12:6

*I*f sleeping well is the outward sign of a solid walk with the
Lord and unwavering faith, then I'm in big trouble. My
sleeplessness started in earnest when Dad had been diagnosed with Alzheimer's yet was still driving his car. He was a night
owl by nature, so about the time we were going to bed, I could
assume Dad was taking to the roads.

I worried that he would get lost, get in a wreck, hurt himself,
or, even worse, hurt someone else. Yes, I prayed, but somehow,
under the veil of night and without the distractions of daily life,
I worried.

That's why the image of Peter sleeping chained between soldiers, on the eve of his trial before an unsympathetic judge, fasci-
nates and humbles me. Peter not only slept; he slept so soundly that
his liberating angel had to give him a pop on his side to wake him
up!

It's not as though Peter didn't realize he faced real danger.
Herod had recently killed James, a fellow believer and follower of
Jesus. The Jews' reaction to this murder was so enthusiastic that
Herod decided he was on a roll and would kill Peter as well. I suspect that somewhere in the recesses of Herod's mind he must have
known he was in over his head by persecuting followers of the One
who worked miracles and claimed to be God. Otherwise, why
would he have found it necessary to lock Peter in a cell, chain him
between two soldiers, and then be further guarded by sentries at
the entrance? One might have thought that Peter must be a violent
and elusive murderer rather than a follower of Jesus.

Herod was probably unaware that the disciples and others were not taking Peter's imprisonment lightly. They were not protesting outside the jail or circulating a petition for Peter's release, but they had the ear of Almighty God and were praying for a miracle.

God must have been pleased with their prayers and with Peter's resting faith, for he sent light into the darkness, an angel to show the way, and he led Peter to the safety of his brothers.

I want this kind of faith.

Heavenly Father,
How I underestimate you! To think that my worry could
accomplish anything other than robbing me of sleep and an
opportunity for you to be Lord and Master of my life. This is
why you've said that worry is a sin. My troubles, rather
than you, become my focus. Forgive me. Let me remember
Peter, chained by circumstances but utterly free in you. Amen.

Psalm for the Soul

Indeed, he who watches over Israel
will neither slumber nor sleep. (Ps. 121:4)

Hope for the Exile

"For I know the plans I have for you," declares the LORD,
*"plans to prosper you and not to harm you, plans
to give you hope and a future."*
JEREMIAH 29:11

*W*hen I was consumed with caring for each of my parents,
I remember saying to my husband, "I don't even recognize my life anymore!" I felt like I was in exile from my
normal routine and the comforting elements that usually comprised
my day. I could no more see God's long-term plan than I could see
oxygen in the air. All I knew was that my day was absorbed with
managing the physical care, emotional support, and the spiritual
needs of my parents. But even when we are exiled from the normal
comforts of our life, there is real hope we can cling to.

When Jeremiah the prophet delivered the precious and comforting words of this passage to the Jews, they were in a literal
exile. King Nebuchadnezzar had taken craftsmen and artisans from
Jerusalem to Babylon for the purpose of using their skills to beautify and advance the city. So the Jews were uprooted from their
normal life, their homes and families. They were not slaves, they
could live as they pleased, but they couldn't return home.
Naturally, they wanted their trial to be over, so they were ripe to
believe the false prophets who told them that soon they would be
going home. As a result, the Jews were living like transients, unwilling to accept their situation as permanent and settle down.

In reality their exile was far from over. God had told Jeremiah
that they would be in Babylon for seventy years. It was imperative,
therefore, that the Jews come to terms with this and go about the
business of marrying, having children, buying property, and planting fields. Otherwise they would eventually be diminished as a race
and culture. This was not what the Jews wanted, but the prophet

assured them that God had not abandoned them. He had a plan for them that gave them a future and hope.

Knowing they were facing a difficult transition, God graciously told them how to cope: "'Then you will call upon me and come and pray to me, and I will listen to you. You will seek me . . . with all your heart. I will be found by you,' declares the LORD, 'and will bring you back from captivity'" (Jer. 29:12–13). The key to their survival and happiness was cleaving to God while making the best of their situation.

When we are in the throes of trials, it is tempting to abandon the things that bring us comfort and stability. We must cling to our confidence that God has a plan for us just as surely as he had a plan for the Jews. When we kick against our circumstances or set about handling things on our own in vain confidence, we are headed for despair. Just as God honored the faithful obedience of the Jews and restored them to their beloved Jerusalem, he will honor our trust and devotion to him through our trial and bring us into glorious restoration.

Dear Lord,
Although my life is difficult right now, make me fully aware of the good and comforting things you have given me. I don't understand your plan for me, but I trust you. I am calling upon you and seeking you with all my heart, knowing you have promised to listen and let yourself be found. In Jesus' name. Amen.

Psalm for the Soul

May your unfailing love rest upon us, O LORD,
even as we put our hope in you.
(Ps. 33:22)

The Source of Strength

I can do everything through him
who gives me strength.
PHILIPPIANS 4:13

*C*aregiving doesn't occur in a vacuum. Other aspects of life continue to go on and require our attention and energy. For me there were several months when the needs of each of my parents overlapped. Despite my attempts to schedule, sometimes the demands of the day required more than I could anticipate.

It was just such a day when I had taken Mom to the hospital for a surgical biopsy. While in the waiting room, I received two calls from Dad's caregiver. He was confused and trying to unlatch the gate and leave. "He's a handful right now," she told me, "and he keeps asking for you. Can you come over and calm him down?"

I explained my situation. "Tell him I'll be there as soon as I can." When I hung up, I mulled over my options: I wouldn't leave Mom until she was safely out of surgery. But then, if all was going well, I could run over and see Dad while she was in the recovery room. If I hurried and Dad was cooperative, I might get him settled and be back to the hospital about the time Mom was waking up. . . . And so went the day.

That night I sank into sleep. I dreamed I was shopping in a warehouse store. My cart was full, and the aisles were narrow. Suddenly, the lights went out. I could hear people around me. Every instinct told me to leave the cumbersome cart and grope my way out of the oppressive darkness, but I couldn't. Who would take care of my full cart? I stood there in the dark, panic growing, and wanting freedom and light more than anything in the world.

Later, when I thought about this dream, I realized it captured my mixed feelings. Between Dad and Mom, my cart was indeed full. And sometimes I wanted to run from it all and just take care of myself.

Thankfully, things weren't always so demanding, but I was surprised by how much strength and endurance were required during a day of caring for my parents. Sometimes the effort was more emotional than physical, but the end of the day usually found me exhausted. Therefore, I was very aware that to do *everything* I needed to do, I had to pray constantly and draw from a source of strength greater than myself.

When Paul wrote that we can do *everything* through Christ who gives us strength, he was referring to those things that are within God's will and purpose for our lives. As we go about the business our heavenly Father wants us to accomplish, he will add to our strength and abilities so that it can reach completion.

How are you holding up to this awesome task of caregiving? The day will come, if it hasn't already, when your energy is depleted. Don't wait until you're on empty to ask God to replenish you with his strength. We can have confidence that when we are about the business of helping our parents through the end of their lives, we are in God's will; therefore, the strength of Christ is available to us.

Heavenly Father,
I need your strength to do this work set before me.
Although I am often exhausted, you are constant in
your refreshing sufficiency. As I answer the responsibility
to help my loved one, transform my weariness to hope
and my discouragement to courage. Amen.

Psalm for the Soul

God is our refuge and strength,
an ever-present help in trouble. (Ps. 46:1)

Homesick for Heaven

Meanwhile we groan, longing to be clothed
with our heavenly dwelling.
2 CORINTHIANS 5:2

During Dad's last year or so, the recurrent and frustrating theme of his life was that he wanted to go home. Ironically, this started when he was still in the house he had lived in for years. He would phone me and ask when he was going to be able to go home. When I questioned him about it, he described a house that existed somewhere just out of sight—just down the block and just around the corner.

When he moved to the group home, he was understandably even more disoriented. Time after time he would call me insisting that he wanted to go home. Again, in his mind, his home was nearby—just out of reach. Often he was angry and threatening to call a cab and go on his own if I wouldn't take him there.

One day, after a series of these phone calls, I wearily said, "Dad, I'm coming over to get you, and you show me where your home is." I knew it was an exercise in futility, but I hoped that maybe by going through the process, he would finally be convinced and lay the issue to rest.

Once he was in the car, I said, "OK, Dad, which way do I go?" With complete confidence he pointed left. At the stop sign I asked again. "Now which way?" He pointed right. In no time at all we had made a convoluted circle through the neighborhood. I could see that he was worried and confused. "I don't understand," he said.

I felt miserable and foolish as I pulled back into the driveway. "Everything's OK, Dad. Don't worry. Let's just go inside, and I'll read for awhile."

Dad reluctantly settled on his bed, and I began to read. After several minutes he quietly interrupted me. "Will I be going home soon?" His voice was as wistful as a child's.

How could I take away his hope? "Yes," I answered with confidence.

I looked down at the book again and resumed reading, not even hearing my own words as I pondered my answer to him. It wasn't a lie. Dad would indeed be going home soon—finally leaving behind the worn and weary tent that had serviced him throughout his life and now imprisoned him with age, disease, and weariness. Soon his groanings and frustrations would come to an end, and he would be forever liberated, joyful, comfortable, and consumed in the worship of his Lord. No longer would he search for a home that eluded him. He would be with the Savior, enjoying perfect peace and perfect rest. He would be home.

"Do you promise?" he whispered.

"Yes, Dad." I bit my lower lip. "I promise."

Heavenly Father,
Nothing brings to mind my eternal home in heaven like
seeing the wasting away of our earthly bodies. Let these
facts of human existence keep my touch on earthly things
light and my hold on heavenly things close to my heart.
In Jesus' name. Amen.

Psalm for the Soul

Surely goodness and love will follow me
all the days of my life,
and I will dwell in the house of the LORD forever. (Ps. 23:6)

One Needed Thing

"Martha, Martha," the Lord answered, "you are worried and upset about many things, but only one thing is needed. Mary has chosen what is better, and it will not be taken away from her."
LUKE 10:41–42

Caregiving is all about meeting needs. So it's understandable to become so focused on tasks and chores that we overlook the most important need: enjoying the presence and company of the one for whom we are caring.

This is an age-old tendency that is completely understandable. Even Martha, who had the great privilege of being in the company of Jesus himself, was not able to sort between tasks and opportunity and choose the better thing.

I sympathize with Martha. Just imagine what it must have been like. Martha had heard that Jesus and his disciples had come to her village. She must have known about Jesus and the many miraculous things he had done, so she opened her home to him and the disciples—a lovely gesture. Martha knew this was no ordinary guest—he claimed to be the Son of God—and she must have wanted to treat him royally. She probably quickly took a mental inventory of what foods she had and how she would prepare them for her special guests. Perhaps she would use her finest serving pieces and take extra care in setting the table. She probably pictured herself and Mary working together to prepare and serve a meal that Jesus and his disciples would long remember.

But things didn't go the way Martha anticipated. Rather than having her sister work at her side, Mary sat enthralled at the feet of Jesus—just as though she were a guest! Martha may have tried to ignore the situation for awhile, but as she furiously worked alone, she became more and more furious with her sister. Finally, she could contain her frustration no longer, so she complained to Jesus. Surely he would see the injustice.

But to her surprise, Jesus didn't agree that Mary was being unfair. Instead, he told Martha that by being concerned about so many things, she had overlooked the most important thing—spending time with him. On the other hand, Mary had chosen Jesus above all else, and the Lord commended her for it.

It's easy to see ourselves in Martha's behavior because it's simply easier to do things for the Lord than to be quiet and attentive in his presence. We might even secretly hope that he would be openly impressed with our efforts, a thinly disguised form of pride, and so much more comfortable than doing the work of seeing ourselves as sinners who desperately need a Savior.

Although spending time with our ailing loved ones cannot be equated with the opportunity to spend time at the feet of Jesus, this valuable portion of Scripture reveals our tendency to choose the lesser thing in our precious relationships. In spite of our loved one's many needs, the greater need is to spend time in his company.

Heavenly Father,
Martha has served as an awesome example to me.
Let me learn from her experience. I want to
choose what cannot be taken away from me—time
with others—and time with you. In Jesus' name. Amen.

Psalm for the Soul

Better is one day in your courts
than a thousand elsewhere. (Ps. 84:10a)

Separation Security

*Who shall separate us from the love of Christ? Shall
trouble or hardship or persecution or famine or
nakedness or danger or sword?*
ROMANS 8:35

Separation anxiety is the fear of being separated from someone we love and the concern that either they or we won't
be OK through the absence. Regardless of whether we are
the one leaving or the one being left, separations can be devastating. It goes without saying that when we are caring for a parent or
loved one with a life-threatening illness, we come face-to-face with
these fears.

Through all the pain and trials that Mom endured in her last
illness, the only thing that brought her to tears was the thought of
being separated from the people she loved. With three great grand-
children toddling around her, she thought about their growing up
and all she would miss. She thought of her beloved older sister, her
grandchildren, nieces, friends, and her children. Heaven with its
unknown joys awaited her, but she understandably mourned leaving the known loves of her life.

In this finite, mortal lifetime, separation is a reality. For
believers in Jesus Christ, however, we live within a larger reality—
the reality of an unbroken oneness with our Lord. Many years ago,
as a new believer, one of my greatest fears was of being separated
from God either because I had fallen away from him or because
I had finally taxed him to the limit of his patience.

It's true that the world consciously and unconsciously con-
spires to separate us from Jesus. And like the believers in the
Scriptures, we are certain to endure trouble, hardships, and persecution for our faith. In some cases believers experience the
extremes of famine, nakedness, and the dangers of violence and
wars, but even these things don't have the power to separate us

from the love of our Savior and the confidence of an eternity in his presence.

This is security that surpasses every conceivable experience. It bridges death with life and transcends the power of the mightiest angel. It exceeds the highest height or the deepest depth and is outside the boundaries of time. When we belong to Jesus, his love binds us to him through any and every circumstance. We are all subject to the separations brought about by death in this phase of our existence, but nothing can separate us from Christ's love. Nothing.

Precious Lord,
I am confronted with being separated from one I love.
Yet I know that even in these circumstances, you will
work all things together for the good. Give me boldness
to share your gospel if that is needed, give me wisdom
to speak of your strong love that carries us from this
life to life eternal, and give me understanding of your
enduring Word so that I can stand in confidence. Amen.

Psalm for the Soul

May your unfailing love be my comfort,
according to your promise to your servant. (Ps. 119:76)

The Great Divide

Therefore God exalted him to the highest place
and gave him the name that is above every name,
that at the name of Jesus every knee should bow,
in heaven and on earth and under the earth,
and every tongue confess that Jesus Christ is Lord,
to the glory of God the Father.
PHILIPPIANS 2:9–11

*I*t wasn't until I became sick myself that I began to see people in one of two categories: sick or well. Prior to that, when I was healthy, this black-and-white distinction didn't occur to me. After all, becoming a caregiver was an *addition* to my already busy life—another hat I wore above and beyond my usual roles and responsibilities as wife, mom, grandmother, writer, editor, and so on.

Being ill, I discovered, is more about subtraction than addition. Suddenly I experienced loss after loss. I could no longer pursue the interests, responsibilities, or pleasures of my life. Most profoundly, my lifelong perception of myself as a healthy person was abruptly altered. I had become a carereceiver; I had become one of the sick.

In my new circumstances it seemed as though one's health was the factor that constituted the "great divide" between people. As real as it may have felt, this distinction was only an illusion. In truth, what appeared to be a retaining wall of difference between the well and the sick was really a line of chalk, for eventually, we are all subject to illness and death.

If the matter of health or disease is not the issue that unites or divides us, what is? The question that transcends all others and can irrevocably divide humanity is both simple and profound: *What is your relationship to Jesus?*

Incredibly, there will be a moment in time when even the gulf between believers and nonbelievers will dissolve. At that time, when Christ appears to the universe, all in heaven and on earth and those who have preceded us in death will join in unanimous homage to him. For the believer this moment will be the fulfillment of the long-anticipated hope of seeing Christ as King, rightfully crowned with glory and honor. For those who have lived in willful unbelief, it will be a time of reluctant recognition that they, too, are subject to his control and accountable to his judgment. They *will* confess that Jesus is Lord; they *will* bow before him in spontaneous reverence, but they will *not* be saved. Tragically, the great divide will find them irrevocably separated from the Lord they can no longer deny.

You may be so deeply involved in caring for someone who is ill that you have neglected considering this important issue. You may feel insulated from the immediacy of accountability to God because you are currently healthy. If so, you are being deceived. In the grand scheme of things, our lives are little more than vapors. Now is the time to acknowledge the name above all names and willingly bow before the Lord. Don't dare risk finding yourself forever on the wrong side of the great divide.

Heavenly Father,
One day the universe will give Jesus the praise and
adoration and respect he deserves as your Son. Help me
make the choice of reverence now. Create in me an
urgency that won't allow substitutes and distractions
to sway my attention from receiving Christ as my Savior.
When the moment comes that Jesus is revealed, I want
to feel utter joy rather than numbing regret.
In Jesus' name. Amen.

Psalm for the Soul

All the ends of the earth
will remember and turn to the LORD,
and all the families of the nations
will bow down before him,
for dominion belongs to the LORD
and he rules over the nations. (Ps. 22:27–28)

The Work of the Heart

Whatever you do, work at it with all your heart, as working for the Lord, not for men, since you know that you will receive an inheritance from the Lord as a reward. It is the Lord Christ you are serving.
COLOSSIANS 3:23–24

*I*n a perfect world we would care for others with no expectation of having our efforts acknowledged or appreciated. Furthermore, in a perfect world, those we care for would recognize our sacrifice and be genuinely grateful and even tell us so occasionally!

Dealing with my own parents was a study in extremes on the subject. Dad was warmly affectionate most of the time. Expressing appreciation was as natural to him as breathing. Because of his Alzheimer's, I often heard his sweet expressions of gratitude over and over for even the small things I did for him. Somewhere in the recesses of Dad's mind, he knew he needed help and that I loved him and was doing what I could for him.

As openly dependent as Dad was, Mom was determined to be independent. As a single woman for forty years, independence was her badge of personal success. Therefore, in spite of the fact that she eventually required my continual assistance to manage her medical and personal needs, Mom couldn't or wouldn't acknowledge my efforts. She was always polite, always said thank you at the end of the day, but she never freely expressed an overall appreciation for my efforts.

I struggled with this. Sometimes I could feel my resentment bubbling just under the surface. One day as I carried groceries and laundry into her home, she flippantly introduced me to one of her neighbors as her slave. In spite of her light tone, I was wounded. She was my mother. I loved her and was doing my best to take care of her with respect and dignity. I felt my efforts were reduced to a silly put-down.

As her illnesses compounded and intensified, my time was dominated by her needs. I felt certain she would acknowledge my ever increasing efforts, but no.

During this time, as I was studying and praying, the Lord made me aware that my heart was not in the right place. My care for Mom had strings attached. I was after something. I wanted an outward show of her love and verbal approval. The Lord made clear that I was to do the work of caring for her with all my heart, but I had to make the object of my efforts the Lord himself. Rather than feeling defeated by this, I was relieved and finally satisfied.

Ironically, after Mom died, many of her friends told me that she often commented to them about how much I did for her and how she appreciated me. It would have been wonderful to hear it from her lips, but I joyfully accept it now as a special gift from the Lord.

Heavenly Father,
Sometimes I have to be uprooted from my expectations
before I turn to you—my always present, always loving
Father. Help me accept the fact that my loved ones are
human and fallible, and so am I. Rather than becoming
bitter by the spoken hurts and the unspoken slights,
turn my heart toward you, and make me better. Amen.

Psalm for the Soul

Test me, O LORD, and try me,
examine my heart and my mind;
for your love is ever before me,
and I walk continually in your truth. (Ps. 26:2–3)

Numbered Days

Teach us to number our days aright,
that we may gain a heart of wisdom.
PSALM 90:12

*R*ecently I studied an actuarial calculator designed to predict financial needs through retirement years. I filled in the answers to several questions, and with a click of the mouse, my life expectancy appeared on the screen: 86.7 years. Although it's just an educated guess, it's strange to see a number in black-and-white staring back at you.

Our human nature may want to avoid thinking about our eventual death, but Scripture encourages us to consider the brevity of life and the certainty of death so we will keep our priorities straight and cultivate wisdom. The psalmist sees that life is filled with trouble and sorrow, and to avoid being overwhelmed with them, he prays that God's love will be the source of his gladness and joy.

Unconsciously we feel that our parents stand as a barrier between death and ourselves. If all proceeds normally, they will die before we do, so until that time we feel somewhat buffered. My father's passing was the first death that really came close to me, and it had the definite effect of making me more aware of my own mortality. Rather than being depressed by this unvarnished truth, I feel surprisingly motivated to make conscious decisions that will carry me through the rest of my life.

At the top of my list of decisions is my desire for a greater commitment and delight in my relationship to the Lord. I know that one day I, too, will stand at the threshold to eternity. I want to be walking so closely with him that our conversation on earth simply continues in heaven.

Next, the psalmist prayed that the Lord would "establish the work of our hands" (90:17). What a blessing to have work that we dedicate and perform to the glory of the Lord. It doesn't matter whether we are formally in the ministry. The earth is the mission field, and our integrity on the job and our love for our fellowman are the believer's calling cards.

Finally, I want to wear my heart on my sleeve when it comes to showing love for my family. At the end of my life, I pray that there will be no need to awkwardly express feelings that have been suppressed by pride or fear.

We've all heard interviews with people who have survived a potentially deadly situation. It is common for them to say that the experience has made them newly thankful for what they have and passionately appreciative of life. For believers, numbering our days can have a similar effect, encouraging us to make the most of our time on earth, while serving as a reminder that heaven draws steadily near.

Heavenly Father,
You know the number of my days just as surely as you
know the number of the stars in heaven. I trust that my
life and death are firmly in your control. I have the joy
and certainty that through Jesus death has lost its sting.
I pray that this certainty will prompt me to make my
life about glorifying you and blessing others until
you call me home. Amen.

Psalm for the Soul

"Show me, O LORD, my life's end
and the number of my days;
let me know how fleeting is my life.
You have made my days a mere handbreadth;
the span of my years is as nothing before you." (Ps. 39:4–5)

A Time to Grieve

"Now is your time of grief, but I will see you again and you will rejoice, and no one will take away your joy."
JOHN 16:22

*L*ike so many times of late, the day had been a roller coaster of dealing with Dad's ups and downs. In the morning he had been agitated and furious, wanting to go home "right now!" Later in the afternoon he was sweetly docile as I read to him. "I *love* the way you read!" he would say periodically. Then, at last, he fell asleep, and I tiptoed from his room and headed home.

It was Christmastime. I hadn't even started my shopping, so after dinner I set out to the mall. The Christmas spirit seemed far away as I listened to carols on the radio. As I pulled into the parking lot, Gene Autry began to sing "Rudolph the Red-Nosed Reindeer." I had never been crazy about that song, but as I listened, something distant and tender tugged at my heart. I could so clearly remember being a little girl and hearing that song. Dad was strong then, effortlessly hoisting the Christmas tree to the roof of the car and expertly tying the ropes to the bumper. He was my hero, my safety, my strong and capable father, and I was his child. He was not to be trifled with. He could correct or comfort me simply by the look on his face. But I knew that he stood between me and the world, and he would not allow me to be harmed.

For some reason that song awakened memories that were all but buried by time and the draining demands of the present day. It touched that part of me that yearned for the simple clarity of being a child to my father, rather than cast into this new and awkward role of caring for him.

I sat there in the dark car, listened to the song from my child-hood, and cried.

Grieving begins long before the actual loss when we are dealing with long-term illness. With every new limitation and every diminished capability, we experience loss and grief. Every time we step in to care for our parent, whether writing out the bills, dealing with the doctors, or helping them shower and dress, we are confronted with the jolting reality of our altered parent-child relationship. And we grieve.

Jesus was a Man well acquainted with grief. He comforted his disciples when he knew the end of his life on earth was near. He knew they would be heartbroken and confused. He comforts us today in just the same way: he assures us that we will see our believing loved one again. And when we do, we will rejoice knowing that illness, age, war, or accident will never again take away our joy.

> *Heavenly Father,*
> *The disciples' faith was challenged when they understood*
> *that you would no longer be with them. I, too, am*
> *challenged to have faith in your Word at this time*
> *of loss. I have to trust in the unseen promise that one*
> *day I will be with my loved one again. Teach me to*
> *grieve without shame but never to grieve as though*
> *I had no hope. In Jesus' name. Amen.*

Psalm for the Soul

But you, O God, do see trouble and grief;
you consider it to take it in hand.
The victim commits himself to you;
you are the helper of the fatherless. (Ps. 10:14)

Runaway Obedience

*Confident of your obedience, I write to you, knowing
that you will do even more than I ask.*
PHILEMON 21

*I*n the New Testament book of Philemon we read about a
man (Philemon) whose slave had run away, perhaps even
stealing a few things as he left. The runaway slave subsequently met the Apostle Paul and became a believer. Now, Paul is
writing Philemon and asking him to accept the man back again not
as a slave but as a brother in the Lord!

When we have been wronged by someone, we can find
ourselves on surprisingly perilous ground. It's a small step from
righteous indignation to actively fostering bitterness and self-
righteousness. This short letter does not tell us how Philemon
reacted to Paul's request, but I wonder if this act of obedience was
difficult for him. After all, Philemon was the injured party. He had
suffered financial loss, the loss of possessions, and now Paul, his
friend and mentor, was asking him to overlook those losses and
receive the runaway back on the equal footing of a fellow believer
in Christ!

How do you react when the Lord asks you to ignore your own
standards of justice and, instead, obey him? Maybe, like myself, the
parent you are caring for was a runaway parent. He or she may
have left the family when you were a child and, in the process, left
you with deep pain, hardships, and heartache. When you needed
him to care for you and be your strength, he was nowhere to be
found. You were treated unfairly—deserted—and now, incredibly,
God has put you in the position of being the person in the family
to be there for him. *This isn't fair!* You might think. *Why should
I obey?*

God's goal with his children is far greater than being fair. By
our obedience he wants to free us from the constraints of long-held

hurts and, in the process, teach us to trust him wholly. There had been a void in my life since Dad left our family. Even though in recent years he and I had become comfortable and friendly, there was just no way of compensating for the deep childhood losses. And then the Lord ordered events in such a way that my dad needed me.

Incredibly, by caring for Dad through his end-of-life illnesses my own losses began to be filled. During this trying time, when I often felt depleted, my faithful heavenly Father was my strength, my source, my comfort, and I was able to give to my dad that which I myself had needed so much when I was young.

Paul knew that Philemon would do even more than he asked. I can't say that my obedience in any way exceeded what God wanted me to do, but I know this: God honored my efforts and gave me back much more than I could have asked.

Father in Heaven,
I know that my own heart was once that of a rebellious
runaway before you found me, paid my debts, and saved
me. Let me put aside the past hurts and have my actions
flow out of trust and the desire to please you. I have
confidence that when hard things come into my life,
you are there as my nurturing Parent urging me
to stretch, heal, and reach maturity. Amen.

Psalm for the Soul
I will hasten and not delay
to obey your commands. (Ps. 119:60)

Tears

Jesus wept.
JOHN 11:35

Crying is one of the last great taboos of our culture. We admire the individual who bravely and quietly endures loss and reserves his grief for the privacy of home. It's interesting that the medical community has discovered that crying is good for us. Tears are a mechanism for healing as they wash away harmful chemicals produced during times of stress.

Although it may be good for us to cry, people try to stop our tears by saying some well-meaning but predictable things such as, "He is in a better place now," or, "Her suffering is over," or, "Don't cry. One day you'll be together again." All these statements may be true, but they inhibit and deprive us of the right and necessity to cry.

As it is, believers continually deal with the paradox of knowing that while death is sad, it is the springboard to heaven and eternal life. We must reconcile that Christian hope with the real and painful losses in this realm of existence.

No one understood better the joys of heaven than Jesus, yet when his dear friend Lazarus died, he was profoundly affected. His compassion extended to all those who were grieving and distraught. "When Jesus saw her [Mary] weeping, and the Jews who had come along with her also weeping, he was deeply moved in spirit and troubled" (John 11:33).

Mary and Martha were grief-stricken over the death of their brother—in part because they knew that had Jesus been there, he could have cured Lazarus's illness. Jesus, however, was not surprised by any of these events. He had purposefully timed his visit to Bethany knowing Lazarus would die and knowing he would raise him from the dead. Yet he wept.

Why would Jesus weep if he knew Lazarus would be in heaven? Perhaps he wept as the all-knowing God who could see the devastating effects of sin and death on the world he created for worship and the sweet fellowship of man with God. Or maybe in his great tenderness, he wept for those who were suffering from the loss. His tears may have been for Lazarus and the pain that preceded his death or the sad truth that one day he would have to die again. Maybe he wept for all these reasons and more.

Whether or not we can know the thoughts that accompanied Jesus' tears, we know with certainty that our God does not dispassionately stand back and clinically observe our pain. He knows our sadness and grief because he has experienced them to a greater degree than we will ever know. The prophet Isaiah said this of him: "He was despised and rejected by men, a man of sorrows, and familiar with suffering" (Isa. 53:3).

Jesus wept, and we will too—but not as those who have no hope. When a believer dies, we have a genuine reason to rejoice, but it's right and understandable to be sad and weep—just as our Savior did.

Heavenly Father,
You care about my tears so much that your Word says
you put them into your bottle and record them in your
book. Thank you for your Son Jesus, who cries with
us even as he saves us. Amen.

Psalm for the Soul

But you, O God, do see trouble and grief;
you consider it to take it in hand.
The victim commits himself to you;
you are the helper of the fatherless. (Ps. 10:14)

Warm and Deadly

"So, because you are lukewarm—neither hot nor cold—
I am about to spit you out of my mouth."
REVELATION 3:16

I have a weakness for coffee latte. I love the rich espresso combined with steamed milk to make a creamy, hot drink. Recently, I had a rude surprise when my drink was accidentally made with lukewarm milk. It was only social conscience that enabled me to choke down that first swallow rather than deposit it on the floor.

Warm can be good: puppies come to mind, as well as summer days and my husband's hand holding mine. However, lukewarm is a deadly spiritual temperature for people who profess to be believers.

Lately, however, our society has decided that when talking about Jesus Christ, we must be careful to present only a lukewarm attitude and devotion to him. In the name of tolerance, if we *must* state our beliefs, we are encouraged to temper our remarks by saying our beliefs are true for ourselves—others may have a different truth. By straddling the fence, we may feel that we've dodged the bullet of being labeled a fanatic, but if our beliefs aren't strong enough to defend, and the truth of Jesus Christ isn't *the* truth, why bother?

That is why in this letter to the Laodiceans, Jesus said he would prefer them to be hot or cold rather than lukewarm. Why would he prefer that they were cold rather than warm? Isn't lukewarm closer to hot than cold? No. In the comfort of being lukewarm, they pridefully saw themselves as rich and felt they required nothing more than they already had. Jesus, however, saw them as they truly were, "wretched, pitiful, poor, blind and naked" (Rev. 3:17). In contrast, the person who is cold toward Jesus knows it. He is honest about his condition, therefore, if he becomes tired of being cold, he will consciously take measures to change his condition.

We can be sure that Satan has planted lies at the root of the lukewarm mind-set. For instance, the lukewarm believer may be harboring false notions, like good works—such as caring for a loved one—will get him to heaven. Or maybe one Sunday he went forward at church and was baptized—that's proof he's a Christian, right? Then there's the notion that if his parents were Christians, he was automatically born into the faith. True? No—all lies.

Having a genuine relationship and being personally "on fire" for Jesus Christ is the only way to please him. Unbelievably, Jesus still humbly and courteously seeks out even the lukewarm individual. "Here I am!" he says, "I stand at the door and knock. If anyone hears my voice and opens the door, I will come in and eat with him, and he with me" (v. 20). That's the Creator of the universe loving and pursuing us! How can we resist?

I guarantee you'll never be satisfied with a lukewarm-latte faith again once you've experienced the sizzling fellowship of dining with Jesus in divine intimacy.

Father God,
I can't bear the thought that my tepid faith nauseates
Jesus. Give me courage to recognize my complacency
and shake off my halfhearted commitment. Instead I want
to love him with a passion and fire that ignites my life
and my faith. Thank you, Father, that you have heard
my prayer. In Jesus' name. Amen.

Psalm for the Soul
I hate double-minded men,
but I love your law. (Ps. 119:113)

Sundown

"In your anger do not sin." Do not let the sun go down
while you are still angry.
EPHESIANS 4:26

*I*f you are one of the blessed individuals who doesn't have
any unresolved anger toward your parent, you can skip the
following devotion. If, however, you are among those of us
struggling to get past anger and resentment, read on.

It seems obvious that the last thing we *want* to feel at this
sad time is anger. Anger is embarrassing, demeaning, and socially
unacceptable, especially when felt toward a dying parent. But
parent/child relationships are complex, and lingering anger usually
has deep and painful roots.

Having said that, the Bible tells us simply that we are not to let
the sun go down on our anger. It doesn't add the exception of
*unless you have a particularly stubborn or willful parent who hurt
you in your youth and continues to vex you to this day.* What, then,
can we do to resolve long-standing issues at this delicate time?

We might wonder how anything could be settled unless or until
our parent asks for our forgiveness. Maybe some inspired words
would finally break the shell of a hard-hearted person, or a
thoughtful gesture might prompt the parent suddenly to see his or
her selfishness. Perhaps if we could just quote the perfect Scripture
at the perfect time, the stubborn unbeliever would finally come to
Christ, repent, and ask forgiveness.

Sounds good, but can we count on any of these scenarios? No.
That's why the Bible doesn't put the conditions for resolving anger
and unforgiveness in the hands of anyone other than ourselves
through the power of God.

Harboring anger and unforgiveness is playing with fire. Satan
uses our anger as a foothold to make us nurture and cherish the

wrongs we have suffered. What began as legitimate righteous anger can become a catalyst for prideful self-obsession.

It helps to remember that when Christ died for us we too were sinful, hardened, selfish, rebellious, prideful, and lost. Jesus didn't wait until we "came around" before doing the work on the cross that could set us free. Therefore, we must come before the Lord and confess our anger toward the parent who wronged us and now needs our help.

It's possible that the Lord may prompt us to confront our parent and tell him or her that we have been hurt. Only God knows whether such an effort would bring healing or more hurt. Regardless of how God leads, out of sheer obedience, we must imitate the forgiveness Christ has shown us—forgiveness that requires nothing from our parent but everything from ourselves. It may not seem fair, but by consciously letting go, life and peace will be gained.

The *sundown* of death will eventually bring an end to the opportunity to deal with your anger while your parent is still alive. He or she may never know you have confessed your anger and sin, but you and God know, and you will live in that liberation forever.

Heavenly Father,
If I am to let go of my anger toward my parent, it will
have to be through your power. It would be wonderful
if my parent would soften and help build a bridge
between us, but I know I can't count on that. I can
only count on the bridge you built between man and
God with your death on the cross. I don't want the
sun to set again before I confess my anger and commit
the resolution of it to you. In Jesus' name. Amen.

Psalm for the Soul

Refrain from anger and turn from wrath;
do not fret—it leads only to evil. (Ps. 37:8)

Promise Thinking

Finally, brothers, whatever is true, whatever is noble,
whatever is right, whatever is pure, whatever is lovely,
whatever is admirable—if anything is excellent or
praiseworthy—think about such things.
PHILIPPIANS 4:8

For well over an hour, I had been on the Internet research-ing Mom's condition, treatment options, and prognosis. With every click of the mouse, I was presented with screen after screen of new information that required thoughtful consider-ation. Suddenly I understood why computers sometimes just up and crash. I felt like that myself. Information overload! I turned off the computer, but it wasn't nearly so easy to turn off my thoughts.

The Lord knows how outside circumstances and our own thoughts can rob us of joy and hope. Worldly wisdom says we have to wait for our circumstances to change before we can feel better and the cloud of depression lifts. At the other end of the spectrum is the ever-popular "positive thinking." It sounds good, but its value rests entirely on the validity and truth of those thoughts. Wouldn't it be much wiser to let go of wistful and contrived *posi-tive* thinking, and instead, steep our minds in solid *promise* think-ing—thoughts that are based on the Word and character of God?

The Holy Spirit through Paul tells us how to take a disciplined approach to the control of our thought-life. One of the first things to notice is that throughout the Bible we are told that we have the ability to control our thought-life. In this passage, Paul enumerates the topics that enable such control.

Our minds are blessed and molded when we contemplate those things that are *true* and reflect well-rounded virtues, *noble* things that are worthy of respect and honor, *just* things that are clearly right in the sight of God and man, *pure* things that are not defiled with evil, *lovely* things that are dear to us, *admirable* things that inspire us to greater goodness, and *excellent* things that reflect strong character and diligence.

These thoughts are worthy of our praise and profitable to think about at any time, in any situation. If they seem vague or hard to retain, the embodiment of all these traits and attributes is found in their fullest form in the character and nature of our Lord Jesus Christ. At any time when our thoughts hold us captive, we can consider Jesus—his loveliness, the truth of his message, his mercy and justice, and the excellence of his noble work on the cross.

Holy Father,
I know that I will never be able to control my thinking
unless I make the firm decision to do so. Strengthen me
to follow my decision with disciplined thoughts and,
finally, with disciplined practices. Even in hard times,
when sad thoughts and grim facts enter my life uninvited,
let me rest my mind on you and the peace of God. Amen.

Psalm for the Soul

For the word of the LORD is right and true;
he is faithful in all he does.
The LORD loves righteousness and justice;
the earth is full of his unfailing love. (Ps. 33:4–5)

Jars of Light

*But we have this treasure in jars of clay to show that this
all-surpassing power is from God and not from us.*
2 CORINTHIANS 4:7

The odds were clearly stacked against them. Under Gideon's
leadership, his army of 300 men was planning an attack on
an army of 135,000! Although it may sound like a doomed
military strategy, God had systematically led Gideon to reduce the
number of his 32,000 fighting men so that Israel would not be able
to credit a military victory to a large and powerful army. It would
be undeniable that this was God's victory. To further dramatize the
situation, each man was armed with the unconventional weaponry
of a trumpet and an earthenware jar with a torch hidden inside.

When the attack commenced, the soldiers blew their trumpets,
broke their jars so that the light shown out of the darkness, and
shouted "For the LORD and for Gideon" (Judg. 7:18). Imagine the
Midianites' shock when the deep darkness and silence of night
were shattered by the discordant blare from three hundred trumpets and the flames of fire that seemed to dance, suspended in mid-
air. The enemy's panic and confusion resulted in a brilliant victory
for Gideon. God had used the improbable, the overwhelmed, the
humble, and the breakable to manifest himself.

And he still does to this day. Only now *we* are the simple jars
of clay that hold the treasure of the light of the gospel. Under the
strain of caring for others, we sometimes feel incapable of speaking
clearly about God's love and his plan to save us for eternity. But
even in times of stress, the light of God's presence in our lives can
manifest in ways we might not consider. The simple acts of placing
a cool cloth on a fevered brow, bringing a loaf of special bread
from a bakery, or writing out checks to pay the monthly bills can
be a divine balm to the one in need. In this practical realm of caring, we become the unleashed light of the gospel.

There is a saying in business management that sums up the relationship of a manager to the staff: "No one cares what you know until they know that you care." This is so true in our relationships with the lives we touch on a daily basis. We don't need to have all the answers or effortlessly to bear the stress of our load in order to have a life that glorifies God. Sometimes, in fact, the only way the light of Jesus can be seen is when the clay pots of our lives crack with strain.

Heavenly Father,
I sometimes wonder if I can hold things together under
the added responsibility of caring for another. Help me
remember that when I am overloaded and out of my depth,
it will be obvious that you are the One to receive any
glory from my small acts of caring and love. Replenish
my spirit daily as I drink from the well of your Word
and seek your Holy Spirit to fill and guide me. Amen.

Psalm for the Soul

You are awesome, O God, in your sanctuary;
the God of Israel gives power and strength to his people.
Praise be to God! (Ps. 68:35)

Providential Circumstances

And everyone went to his own town to register.
LUKE 2:3

To the casual observer, it just seemed like bad timing. Caesar Augustus, the Roman emperor, had issued a decree to the Roman world requiring everyone to return to his home-town so that a census could be taken. For Joseph and Mary, however, it could not have come at a worse time. Mary's baby was due, but the decree could not be ignored; they had to make the uncomfortable journey from Nazareth to Bethlehem.

Much more was going on in these circumstances than met the eye. Caesar Augustus only appeared to be in control of events while, in reality, he was a pawn in the providential plan of God. By requiring Mary to return to Bethlehem, his decree unknowingly contributed to the fulfillment of the Old Testament prophecy of the Lord's birth: "But you, Bethlehem Ephrathah, though you are small among the clans of Judah, out of you will come for me one who will be ruler over Israel, whose origins are from of old, from ancient times" (Mic. 5:2).

We talk about coincidence, luck, and even serendipity, but *providence* can be a fuzzy concept. The *New Webster's Dictionary* defines it as: "Foreseeing needs and making provision to supply them; prudent in preparing for future urgencies." I believe that God, while working all things together for good, guides our life providentially more than we can imagine. Once in a great while, the curtain is pulled back, and our Father allows us to see his hand at work through the most mundane of circumstances. He graciously gave me such a glimpse when I was caring for my father.

During the last few months of Dad's life, I read several books to him. He particularly enjoyed one book that reminded him of his childhood on the farm in East Texas. Usually, he became so involved in the story that he was able to forget his cares and relax.

One afternoon, however, Dad was particularly restless. I read for over an hour before he fell asleep. At that point I could have closed the book and left as I usually did. On that day, however, I just wanted to be with him, so I continued reading out loud for another hour as he slept.

The next morning when I got to the group home, one of the caregivers met me at the door. "He's dying, Laura," she said. As I rushed to his room, I didn't know what to expect, but I found him awake, able to whisper he loved me and kiss my hand. I hugged him and prayed with him. He was restless, so I did what I always did; I read to him. A few hours later, I finished the last page of the last chapter and closed the book. "We've finished the book, Dad," I said. He didn't respond. Within minutes, as I sat beside him, he peacefully slipped from this life and into the presence of the Lord.

If I hadn't read to him while he slept the day before, the book would not have been finished. I can't explain why it was so important to me, but I believe that a loving God had providentially ordered circumstances so that Dad and I could have the gift of sweet completion.

Holy Father,
Your hand is in the small things in my life, so that
your purposes can be fulfilled in the big things. You
ordered the steps of Mary and Joseph as they fulfilled
the prophecies of old, and you will order my steps as
well. As I care for my parent or loved one, I pray that
you will providentially work out your plan for us both.
Amen.

Psalm for the Soul

I cry out to God Most High,
to God, who fulfills his purpose for me. (Ps. 57:2)

A Glimpse of Heaven

After this I looked, and there before me was
a door standing open in heaven.
REVELATION 4:1

When my husband and I take evening walks, I love looking into the houses along the way. With just a glance, I can get a feeling for the atmosphere of a home. Sometimes the ghostly flashing of the TV in a dark room can look cold and lonely, and other times the warmly lit rooms seem to beckon with friendly comfort.

The view of heaven we glimpse from the Bible has tantalized readers through the ages. Dad and I often talked about it and tried to picture what it would be like. "Do you think the streets will really be paved with gold?" he would ask. He loved to think about the majesty of heaven with its transparent, golden streets and the twelve gates, each made of a single pearl. These peeks of heaven were enough to start our imaginations running: What will worship be like? Will we all have beautiful voices? Where will we live (maybe we will be neighbors!)? Could we talk with the apostle Paul, jog with Samson, cook with Martha? In the cool of the day, will we stroll by a sea of crystal with the Lord Jesus? With his arm around our shoulder, will he tell us the mysteries of the universe, show us the times when he invisibly ordered our steps, and relate the joy he felt when we confessed our sins and gave him our heart?

Dad and I both knew that before he would walk through that doorway to heaven, he would have to pass through the corridor of death. But our conversations kept heaven and its wonders in the foreground, even though our fears of the unknown mysteries of death were also present.

Corrie Ten Boom, who survived the horrors of a Nazi concentration camp during WWII, once said, "Never be afraid to trust an unknown future to a known God." During her imprisonment, she had no idea what the future held for her. But she lived with hope and love because she knew God and knew that her eternal future was secure.

Even as believers, we sometimes fear the future. Perhaps our anxieties are not entirely due to ignorance of what's around the corner but the sad fact that we have inadequate knowledge of the nature and character of God. The biblical descriptions of heaven stretch our imaginations and our ability to picture what we have no words to describe. But if our glimpse of heaven is a bit blurry, we can vividly see God's character through the Person of his Son. The centerpiece of heaven will be the throne, and the One sitting on it will be the Almighty Ruler of the universe: Jesus.

Heavenly Father,
I want to bring the hope and reality of heaven closer
to my loved one. Help me talk with ease and joy
about the glimpses of heaven you have given in your
Word. But even more important, I want to know you
so deeply and love you so purely that every conversation
will give you glory and honor and whet our appetite
for heaven. In Jesus' name. Amen.

Psalm for the Soul

I lift up my eyes to you,
to you whose throne is in heaven. (Ps. 123:1)

Praying for an Overcoming Death

*For everyone born of God overcomes the world. This is the
victory that has overcome the world, even our faith.
Who is it that overcomes the world? Only he who
believes that Jesus is the Son of God.*

1 JOHN 5:4–5

As caregivers to our parents, I believe one of our most solemn privileges and responsibilities is to pray that they will have an *overcoming* death. By "overcoming," I mean a death that culminates in eternal life because our parent has had a new birth in Christ.

We should never doubt the appropriateness of praying for our loved one's spiritual condition, but we need to remember that it is the Holy Spirit that draws that person and brings the conviction of the need for salvation. This is a time when it may be possible to lead but not to push.

Even though our prayers are crucial, in order to pray with wisdom, we have to discern the spiritual temperature of our loved one. Of course, the most direct way to this knowledge is to talk openly about spiritual matters, but often this is easier said than done. If such discussions have not been part of our existing relationship, initiating them now can seem awkward and intimidating.

You will probably determine that your parent is in one of three places:

1. from all appearances, estranged from God;
2. holding confused or faulty views; or
3. securely related to the Savior and ready to meet him.

For the parent who is estranged from God, now is a time to pour on the prayer and create lots of openings for discussion. Even if the individual has historically been uninterested in matters of the soul, the disappointments of aging and illness may have created a new hunger and receptivity. The biggest obstacle, oddly, may be our own opinion that the individual will never deviate from long-held attitudes and opinions. Even when someone seems hopelessly alienated, as long as there is breath, it's not too late to overcome eternal separation from God.

Confused or faulty views can be trickier. In such matters we must be careful not to win the battle only to lose the war. There are many issues on which believers may differ that are not matters that should cause division. Rather than point out the flaws of his or her beliefs, start fresh, use the Bible as the authority, and keep focused on Jesus.

If you are confident that your parent is a believer, you truly have cause to rejoice in the midst of sorrow. Both of you know that this life is secondary to the life that is to come. And while death and separation are facts, for believers they are not final but have been gloriously overcome by the death and resurrection of our Lord Jesus Christ.

Dear Lord,
My parent's spiritual condition is of great concern
to me. Even late in life the world, the flesh, and the
devil conspire to draw our attention away from facing
eternity. In spite of that, my faith is in the fact that
Jesus is the Son of God. Therefore, give me wisdom
and courage to seize any opportunity that may arise,
and boldly profess forgiveness of sins and salvation
in Christ. Amen.

Psalm for the Soul

Our God is a God who saves;
from the Sovereign LORD comes escape from death. (Ps. 68:20)

The God of Hope

May the God of hope fill you with all joy and peace
as you trust in him, so that you may overflow with hope
by the power of the Holy Spirit.
ROMANS 15:13

For several weeks I had been watching Mom's blood test results and noticing a disturbing change. On top of a recent major surgery, she continued with a grueling regimen of transfusions and shots to raise her red and white blood counts. Then, suddenly, over a period of just a few weeks, she had gone from an exceptionally low white blood count to a dramatically escalated count that far exceeded normal levels. I hadn't said anything to Mom, but I suspected that she was developing leukemia.

A few weeks later, while in the hospital for another problem, her doctor came to her room and told us that she had advanced leukemia. Mom asked if there was any treatment that might help. The doctor sadly shook her head, "At this point, the disease is advancing so rapidly, there's really no hope."

While it was true that less than a month later Mom would be with the Lord, it was not at all true that there was no hope. In fact, it is in the face of death that our deepest hopes come into sharp realization.

When we finally face the inevitability of death, we resign ourselves to turn away from other sources of hope: the medical specialist, new treatments, experimental drugs, and the like. Now our gaze turns fully toward the Source of eternal hope, the wellspring of life that cannot be corrupted or ruined by a world contaminated by sin and death.

Because our hope is future directed, we are left with the problem of coping with our pain and losses now. Like stars that shine out of the deep night, we have a clearer perspective of life and salvation as circumstances bring us to the dark edge of loss. We are witnessing the fulfillment of the promise that went into effect with the death and resurrection of Jesus Christ. With this certainty comes joy and peace that supernaturally coexist with sadness and grief.

In the sixteenth century the English poet John Donne wrote, "Every man's death diminishes me." For believers the opposite is also true: every believer's death enlarges our view of life and faith and gives shape to our hopes of salvation for eternity.

> *Heavenly Father,*
> *You are the God of hope, because you unlocked*
> *the prison of eternal separation and gave us the*
> *keys to life through the death of your Son. In this time*
> *of sorrow, I need to remember the joy and peace that*
> *cannot be disturbed by circumstances. By the power of*
> *your Holy Spirit, I ask for overflowing hope.*
> *In Jesus' name. Amen.*

Psalm for the Soul

But the eyes of the LORD are on those who fear him,
on those whose hope is in his unfailing love,
to deliver them from death
and keep them alive in famine. (Ps. 33:18–19)

Clear-Minded Prayer

The end of all things is near. Therefore be clear minded
and self-controlled so that you can pray. Above all, love each
other deeply, because love covers over a multitude of sins.
1 PETER 4:7–8

*I*magine kissing your spouse good-bye one morning and hurrying out the door to catch a business flight. After the rush to park the car and get to the gate, you settle into your seat and take a deep breath. In a few minutes you bring out your laptop and decide to get a little work done. It's a routine you've followed dozens of times before—nothing out of the ordinary. But suddenly routine is shattered. Three men are shouting, brandishing knives, and one man says he has a bomb strapped around his waist. Their intentions become shockingly clear: they are hijacking the plane to accomplish a suicide mission against the United States. In an instant everything has changed. The business meeting vanishes from your mind. You think of your spouse, your children, and then you realize that the stakes are greater than just your life and the other lives on the plane; the security of the entire country is threatened. Through cell phone conversations, passengers have learned that other planes have already crashed into the World Trade Centers and the Pentagon. What target is planned for this plane? With sickening realization you begin to understand that your life is about to end, and that other lives may depend on your actions. What do you do?

Todd Beamer prayed. And because he was a man for whom praying was a regular part of life, he knew his heavenly Father and was familiar with praying and seeking God's will for his life. For thirty-two-year-old Todd Beamer, "the end of all things" was at hand. Knowing this, he was able to kneel before God and then stand in the face of unimaginable fear. He was able to love unseen thousands of people so deeply that he took heroic steps to thwart an evil plan in hopes of saving them. He was able to be self-controlled when everything around him was out of control.

In times of crisis, we don't want to have to introduce ourselves to God. This is the problem with the foxhole prayer—praying only when we are in need. Panic tends to rule, and we will not be able to think clearly or to have an understanding of God's will. But when we are established in our fellowship with God, we have a framework within which to talk and to listen to him. It's inevitable that hard times will come, but when they do, we'll be able to look confidently to our God and pray.

Lord,
I don't know when "the end of all things" will be near
for me or for those I love. But as I care for those who
need me now, I want to develop the habit of clear-
minded prayer so that I will be ready for whatever
comes my way. Help me conquer complacency with
devotion and make prayer and fellowship with
you my all in all. Amen.

Psalm for the Soul
Hear my prayer, O LORD;
let my cry for help come to you. (Ps. 102:1)

Remembrance

Remember Jesus Christ, raised from the dead,
descended from David.
2 TIMOTHY 2:8

O n Mother's Day, after many difficult days, Mother went to be with the Lord. For weeks following the funeral, every time I thought of Mom, I remembered her long struggle with illness and the trying circumstances of her death. I privately wondered if I would ever be done recalling those sad events and able to look back on happier times and sweeter memories.

One day I sat in my backyard reading and relaxing. I set my book down and closed my eyes, letting the rumble of a nearby lawn mower coax a distant memory to mind. I recalled a long-ago summer's day when I was so young that Mother stopped my play and led me indoors to the quiet and cool of my room. The chenille bedspread was pulled back, and I climbed up on the bed, protesting all the while. Mom listened, smiled, brushed my bangs off my forehead and kissed my sweaty brow. Her shoes had little stars on them, and I watched them disappear behind the gently closing door as she rejoined the galaxy of grown-ups. I was determined not to nap, but the lawn mower's hum and the expanding white ribbon of jet smoke in the sky outside my window finally wooed me from my cares, and I slept.

Such a humble remembrance, yet one that represented the countless sweet moments of her mothering—the thousands of gentle touches on my life. That recollection finally broke through the barrier of the memory of the harsh circumstances of her death.

The disciples must have wondered if they would ever remember anything other than the horrendous image of the Lord they loved hanging grotesquely from the cross. No one has ever had a more unjust or cruel death than Jesus. The memory must have dominated their thoughts and haunted their dreams.

TWICE *B*LESSED

Paul was imprisoned in Rome and knew that his own death was drawing near when he wrote his second letter to Timothy. He sustained himself and encouraged other believers to remember foremost that Jesus was the long-awaited Messiah—the Christ—from the seed of David, not a tortured man hanging from a tree but the gloriously risen Lord. He conquered death, paid the penalty for our sin, ascended to take his rightful place in the kingdom at the right hand of God the Father, and in doing so, changed our eternity.

We who have trusted Jesus as our Savior have died with him so that we might also live with him (2:11). This seeming paradox carries with it a sublime promise and a shining hope! No matter how harsh the disease, or how cruel the death, remember that glorious life awaits those who have put their trust in him—an empowering remembrance.

Heavenly Father,
Through your Word, I can "remember" the compassionate
hands of Jesus as he healed the leper, washed the
disciples' feet, or gathered the little children close to
him. You have the ability to transform painful memories
and make them useful rather than destructive. Help me
lovingly remember those who precede me in death. Amen.

Psalm for the Soul

I will remember the deeds of the LORD;
yes, I will remember your miracles of long ago. (Ps. 77:11)

A Greater Reality

*Jesus said to her, "I am the resurrection and the life. He who
believes in me will live, even though he dies; and whoever lives
and believes in me will never die. Do you believe this?"*
JOHN 11:25–26

Although I knew it was coming, I was truly shocked by the
finality of my parents' deaths. Up to that point even serious illness had coexisted with life. Indeed, it was life that
was the most basic common denominator between my parents and
me. Immediately following their deaths, the reality began to sink in
and was reinforced as I began the process of choosing music and
Scriptures for the services. With every new decision and arrange-
ment, the facts settled deeper into my understanding and became
more real.

Knowing how I felt at these times, it's easy for me to empathize
with Martha's mind-set following the death of her brother,
Lazarus. She and her sister, Mary, had sent word to Jesus when
Lazarus became ill. Yet Jesus didn't arrive at their home until
Lazarus had been buried for four days. Four days after a burial,
every possible hope for recovery and healing had vanished. The
arrangements had been made, the body prepared, and the burial
accomplished.

When Martha saw Jesus, she made clear that she knew he
could have healed Lazarus if he had been there. Without realizing
it, Martha had just revealed what she believed to be Jesus' limitation: he could heal a sick person, but overcoming death would
surely be outside his power.

Through this incident Jesus was intent on showing her, his disciples, and the Jews that death posed no restriction for him. So
when he told Martha that *he* was the resurrection and the life,
he was leading her away from the confines of her experience and

opinion and directing her to consider him, his power, and his position as the Son of God.

With her eyes now on Jesus rather than the sealed tomb of her brother, her faith shown through: "'Yes, Lord,' she told him, 'I believe that you are the Christ, the Son of God, who was to come into the world'" (John 11:27).

As final as death seems to us now, we have only to look to the resurrection of Jesus and his promise of eternal life for believers. Death is a reality in this world, but resurrection for believers in Jesus is a far greater reality.

Heavenly Father,
Like Martha, I impose my limitations on your power,
your love, and your blessings in my life. If I follow the
wisdom of the world, I will look at death as the end
and the point at which our relationships cease. But you
have promised and shown us by example that the
greater reality is your power as the Son of God. You
are the resurrection and the life, and our eternal life
is safe with you. In Jesus' name. Amen.

Psalm for the Soul

Surely goodness and love will follow me
all the days of my life,
and I will dwell in the house of the LORD forever. (Ps. 23:6)

Alone with God

"You will leave me all alone. Yet I am not alone,
for my Father is with me."
JOHN 16:32

*A*t times it seems that the job of caring for our parents will
never end. The Family Caregiver Alliance states that the
average woman will spend seventeen years raising children and eighteen years caring for elderly parents. Sometimes
these roles overlap, creating what is known as "the sandwich generation." The individual in the position of the "bologna" between
these enormous slices of responsibilities can feel suffocated.

In spite of the sobering statistics, the fact is that one day caregiving for our aging parents *will* come to an end. For those who
have devoted years to this effort, it may be a shock. At such times
of loss, we tend to keep our condolences simple, but the fact is that
death often brings an unexpected and confusing array of emotions.
For instance, you may simultaneously feel relief that your loved
one's suffering is over, guilt that your life will now be simpler, deep
sorrow, and profound loneliness.

Jesus experienced loneliness like no human being ever has or
will. As he faced the public enmity of trial and the approaching
reality of the cross, he knew that his disciples would desert him out
of fear and weakness. And then there was the separation that his
ascension would inevitably bring.

Before the disciples left him, the Lord wanted them to know
that despite their abandonment, he would not be alone, "for my
Father is with me." In supreme kindness and compassion, Jesus
told them this in advance so that later they could think of him and
feel peace rather than guilt and regret. They would need the faith
that came from remembering his words because as followers of
Christ, they were bound to face trouble in the world. Jesus
addressed this with touching reassurance when he said, "In this

world you will have trouble. But take heart! I have overcome the world" (John 16:33). Still, in spite of Jesus' efforts, the disciples were stunned by his death on the cross.

In our day it's still a shock to be left. When our parents are gone, we may feel at a loss to know where we will find strength, comfort, or a loving presence to ease our loneliness. We will find them just where Jesus did—in God, our Father.

In your grief and loss, the Lord offers you the same peace and confidence he offered the disciples. One day he will reign supreme over this troubled world beset with sin, sadness, and death. In the meantime, draw close to him in your grief. He understands perfectly. There is no reason to face your loss alone. He has not left you on your own; he has promised to be with you always, even to the end of the age (Matt. 28:20).

Heavenly Father,
I know that Jesus never asks me to go through anything
by myself in my own power. As I try to comprehend
this loss, I want to look to you as my comfort and
strength. It will take time to come to grips with
the realities, regrets, and loneliness that I now feel.
Be with me as you've promised. Through this time,
I want to draw closer to you. In Christ's name. Amen.

Psalm for the Soul

Though my father and mother forsake me,
the LORD will receive me. (Ps. 27:10)

CARERECEIVER DEVOTIONS

The Gift of Knowing

*"And I'll say to myself, 'You have plenty of good things laid up
for many years. Take life easy; eat, drink and be merry.'"*
LUKE 12:19

Would you be able to recognize a precious gift if it came wrapped in an unexpected package? In this parable the rich man had been blessed with an abundance of crops. Unfortunately, what could have been a true blessing filled this man with a false sense of security just as surely as his barns overflowed with grain. In the circumstances of plenty, he had become self-satisfied, overconfident, and indulgent. To his way of thinking, the presence of earthly wealth was so reliable that it blinded him to his own mortality and the condition of his eternal soul!

But the Lord viewed it quite differently "You fool!" he said, "This very night your life will be demanded from you" (v. 20). What good would mountains of grain and an abundance of food and drink do him now?

Sometimes we can see that life is running short. Could this knowledge be called a gift? If so, it is surely bittersweet. I suspect that had the rich man known what the future held, he would have quickly taken stock and rearranged his priorities. For instance, had he affirmed his love for his family? Had he tied up the loose ends of broken relationships? Had he lived generously, giving to the poor according to his abundance? Most importantly, did he know and love the Lord?

I expect he would have concentrated less on amassing goods and much more on amassing unseen riches with the Lord had he known that his earthly possessions did nothing to solve the poverty of his soul.

The concerns and routines of life can have the dulling effect of making us oblivious to our true needs. On the morning of September 11, 2001, thousands of people awoke from their sleep

and went to work, following the routine that must have comprised many other mornings of many other uneventful days. But this was a day like no other. On this day their souls were required of them. Some of them were ready, and certainly some of them were not. Death did not announce itself, but it came just as surely.

For every person the question is not *whether* our soul will be required of us, but whether we will be prepared and ready *when,* at any time, it will be required. Don't be lulled by the apparent sameness of daily life. Now is the time to look past this earthly existence and make sure you have amassed the eternal riches and true security of knowing Christ.

Dear Lord,
Thank you for understanding how easily I can confuse
earthly security with true well-being. Under the shadow
of illness, I want my eyes on you as never before. I confess
that this feels like the loneliest place in the world, yet every
person alive will ultimately reach this point unless you
return first for your church. Fill me with a desire to build up
riches in knowing you. If I've failed to live with this level
of commitment in my life up to now, let me learn now
and finish with it. In Jesus' name. Amen.

Psalm for the Soul

I rejoice in following your statutes
as one rejoices in great riches. (Ps. 119:14)

Hidden Jewels

*For you died, and your life is now
hidden with Christ in God.*
COLOSSIANS 3:3

*Y*ears ago we heard stories of a glamorous movie star who was known for her love of diamonds. She treasured her vast collection of valuable jewelry so much that she did not want to risk having them stolen by wearing them in public. She solved her dilemma by having rhinestone duplicates made of many of her favorite pieces. When she appeared in public, no one knew if she was wearing the genuine diamonds or the paste counterfeits.

This kind of problem is foreign to most of us who don't own anything of such incredible value, but it's interesting to observe how this woman's treasure prompted her to extraordinary measures of protection. Not only did she spend a great deal of energy fretting about the possibility of loss; she also spent untold amounts of money on the counterfeits. Ironically, these cautious measures required the genuine diamonds to sit in the darkness of a vault deprived of the light that would ignite their sparkling fire. We might conclude that while she succeeded in ensuring the safety of her jewels, she defeated the fulfillment of their purpose and deprived herself of enjoying them.

Our Lord faced a much greater challenge in his desire to protect the treasure of his followers. Rather than seeking to avoid personal loss, Jesus walked straight into the ultimate sacrifice—and with radiant results. To give us abundant life here on earth and protect us throughout eternity, he gave absolutely everything at the cross; he gave his sinless life.

As believers, when we placed our faith in Jesus, we also experienced a death. We said good-bye to our "old life" of habitual sin and self-absorption, and we were quietly resurrected into a new life that is held in the protective hand of God.

This is the hidden life, and it is comprised of vast dimensions hidden from the casual observer. In that hidden place we find nourishment through God's Word and the refreshment of the living water of his love. We offer prayers that join us in a hidden communion of our spirit with the Spirit of God. Our hidden life is not a vague facsimile of the Christian life, but the essence of a genuine and eternal relationship.

In some ways we are like those diamonds hidden away in the vault, but unlike those lifeless stones, we have the continual joy and privilege of being bathed in the brilliant life-giving light of the Savior.

Dear Lord,
Thank you for providing me with a hidden sanctuary
of security and peace. The world presses in on me in
so many ways: diminishing health, loss of independence,
pressure from those who don't care and even from
those who do. Let my hidden life flourish in the face
of all that withers and fades. And on that day when hope
becomes reality and someday becomes today, reveal to me
all that has been hidden, and let me look into the
sparkling jewels of your eyes. Amen.

Psalm for the Soul

Keep me as the apple of your eye;
hide me in the shadow of your wings. (Ps. 17:8)

The First Resort

*Hezekiah turned his face to the wall and prayed to the
LORD, "Remember, O LORD, how I have walked
before you faithfully and with wholehearted devotion
and have done what is good in your eyes."*

2 KINGS 20:2–3

*A*ll we can do now is pray."

How many times have we heard that line in television dramas
or movies? The implication is that after all other practical and reliable steps have been taken and have failed, we might as well turn
to the last resort of prayer.

When King Hezekiah fell deathly ill, he saw the power of
prayer quite differently. As a godly and effective king of Judah, the
prophet Isaiah came to him with a word from the Lord: "This is
what the LORD says: Put your house in order, because you are going
to die; you will not recover" (Isa. 38:1). Immediately Hezekiah
turned to God with a passionate plea for life: "Remember, O LORD,
how I have walked before you faithfully and with wholehearted
devotion and have done what is good in your eyes" (v. 3). Hezekiah
obviously loved life and prayed fervently for it. He realized that
when he was in the grave he would be unable to praise God, hope
for his faithfulness, or pass on to younger generations the goodness
of the Lord. These are the pursuits of the living.

The Lord heard his prayer. Before the prophet Isaiah had left
the courtyard, the Lord told him to turn around and deliver
another message to Hezekiah: God had granted him fifteen more
years of life!

In view of this incident, we might be inclined to wonder: If
our prayers can change the mind of God, how can he be truly

sovereign? Wouldn't changing his plan for one's death mean that the plan was not perfect, and, therefore, God is not all-knowing?

Not at all. The Bible tells us over and over to pray without ceasing (1 Thess. 5:17), that the prayer of a righteous man is effective (James 5:16), and that we have not because we fail to ask (James 4:2). Therefore, I believe that within God's sovereign will for us, there is ample room for our prayers to alter the means without disturbing in the least God's overall perfect plan and purpose.

Don't wait until you are standing at the brink of death to pray. Go now to your Father in heaven and pour out your tears and your heart. Like King Hezekiah, have confidence that God will not put you through anything in life or death that is not for your benefit. Whether you are granted more hours, days, months, or years or whether God, in his all-powerful, all-knowing grace, takes you home, that is up to God. But you can have confidence and know that it is right and good to pray for life.

Heavenly Father,
I have such a meek perception of the power of prayer!
If only I knew what was happening in the heavenly realms
when I come to the throne of grace. Are angels being
dispatched on my behalf? Are events being subtly reordered?
Are "coincidences" taking place that will usher in your
blessings? Is a miraculous healing at work in my body?
Make me bold and confident to come to you immediately
with my cares and to trust you completely with the answers.
In Jesus' name. Amen.

Psalm for the Soul

Listen to my cry for help,
my King and my God,
for to you I pray. (Ps. 5:2)

Living in the
There and Then

Set your minds on things above, not on earthly things.
COLOSSIANS 3:2

According to the wisdom of the world, we are told that in order to live life to the fullest, we must avidly "live in the here and now." Those who strive to live this way believe that wringing the last drop of pleasure from each day and "sharing positive energies" with others are the highest contributions they can make to themselves and to the world. In truth, this kind of philosophy is but a shallow attempt to make a selfish and shortsighted existence appear profound. With such meager objectives, there is no reason to search for the purpose of life much less for a deeper relationship with God.

The argument would certainly be made that "now" is all we ever really have and, indeed, that makes perfect sense to those who believe this physical life is all there is. If now is all there is, why grieve about past actions regardless of the pain we may have caused? Why think of future generations and seek to leave a legacy of faith and wisdom? Why think about tomorrow at all when the only certainties are aging and death?

Once again, as believers in Jesus Christ, we find ourselves crossways with the world. Our attachment to this life is tempered with the certainty that it is but the tip of the iceberg. We live with hope and joy not because we are squeezing the last drop of pleasure from the day but because we see that now is our opportunity to please and glorify God.

When we "set our minds on things above," we cultivate a deeply rooted love for heavenly things; we study about them and allow our hearts to be saturated and enthralled by them. With our minds set on eternity, we come into a divine perspective on today.

Our lives are intensely important and will have far-reaching effects on ourselves and those whose lives we touch. But we know that today is not the end result nor the end reward.

It's been said that one can be "so heavenly minded that he is no earthly good." I disagree. When we are truly heavenly minded, we actively strive to put to death our earthly nature and rid ourselves of anger, malice, slander, filthy language, lying, and all types of immorality. Instead, we clothe ourselves with compassion, kindness, humility, gentleness, patience, forgiveness, and love. How could such a heavenly perspective do anything but bring blessings to a hurting world?

Living in the "there and then" means living gracefully and with love today because we know that in AD 30, Christ died for us so that we might receive him as Savior and live with him for eternity. Until *then* we will live with hope and certainty of one day being *there* with him in heaven.

Father in heaven,
I love thinking about heaven and about you. As a believer,
help me cultivate a mind that hungers for what lies ahead.
With this perspective, I pray that it will be obvious that
my life is not a frantic holding on to existence on this plane
but a time of growing in my knowledge of you so that
I can live in hope and pass it on to others.
In Jesus' name. Amen.

Psalm for the Soul

Be exalted, O God, above the heavens,
and let your glory be over all the earth. (Ps. 108:5)

Chain Reactions

*About midnight Paul and Silas were praying and singing hymns
to God, and the other prisoners were listening to them.*
ACTS 16:25

Anyone can sing God's praises when enjoying good health,
personal freedom, and basic human comforts. At such
times we happily agree with God that we are getting just
what we deserve. But what happens when we're shackled to a serious illness or imprisoned by physical limitations? How can we be
a useful influence from the confines of our home, hospital bed, or
a room in a nursing home?

Maybe you think that because of your weakened physical
health, God has taken you out of the game and placed you on the
sidelines of life and usefulness.

Think again.

Paul and Silas had been going about their business as mission-
aries for Christ when they came under the fire of false accusations
motivated by greed. Suddenly they were snatched away from their
plans, severely beaten and thrown into the *inner* cell of the prison
with their feet clamped in stocks. The isolated inner cell may have
been more like a dungeon with perpetual darkness; damp, slimy
walls and clammy cold. It was the cell reserved for the worst of the
worst prisoners.

What could they possibly do to get out of the prison and continue their mission? Did they hatch a clever plan to distract the
guard and steal his keys? Did they make a phone call to the best
lawyer in Philippi? No. Paul and Silas did the same things they
probably would have done if they were camping around a fire or
in the home of friends: they prayed and sang hymns!

And what a response! God shook the foundations of the prison
with an earthquake. The doors flew open and the chains broke
free. When the jailer saw the open doors, he felt certain that the

prisoners would have seized the opportunity and fled. So he prepared to kill himself rather than be killed for failing his assignment.

Then, out of the pitch darkness, he heard Paul shout, "Don't harm yourself! We are all here!" (v. 28).

When the jailer called for lights, incredibly there sat Paul and Silas in their open cell! In the presence of such holy behavior, the guard's own sin confronted him. Trembling, he fell down before them and asked what he had to do to be saved. His conversion was the first link in a chain reaction that resulted in all of the family members of his household also coming to Christ.

Regardless of our health and circumstances, we should never doubt that our consistent acts of prayer and worship have the potential of influencing others. There is simply no way to measure the power of a humble life in which Jesus Christ is Lord. God may not rattle the foundations of your room with an earthquake, but by your faithful acts he just may shake the foundations of a nearby searching heart.

Heavenly Father,
I often feel powerless—like a prisoner of my illness.
Remind me that my restrictions don't limit you or
your will. Give me courage to live my Christian life
simply, visibly, and in obvious devotion to you.
And then, let your Holy Spirit do its wondrous
work and create a chain reaction of love. Amen.

Psalm for the Soul

Sing joyfully to the LORD, you righteous;
it is fitting for the upright to praise him. (Ps. 33:1)

Reconciled to Righteousness

We are therefore Christ's ambassadors, as though God were making his appeal through us. We implore you on Christ's behalf: Be reconciled to God. God made him who had no sin to be sin for us, so that in him we might become the righteousness of God.

2 CORINTHIANS 5:20–21

For years following my parents' divorce, Dad and I had a difficult and painful relationship. Eventually the fragile ties broke all together, and we were estranged. The separation broke my heart. My efforts to reconcile were rejected, so I did my best to turn my focus to my husband and our young children rather than the hole that Dad's absence left.

On a winter evening six years later, the phone rang. It was Dad. "I'd like to get together with you and talk." I was at once numb and flooded with emotion. For almost as long as I could remember, he had been a source of upset and sorrow. As much as I loved him, my life was peaceful, and I wasn't at all sure I wanted to risk that for a relationship with him. Judging from the past, I wondered how long would it be until something made him mad and he was gone again. And then there were the children. Would they become attached to him only to suffer if he suddenly disappeared?

I talked with my husband and prayed about it for several days before I agreed to meet with him for coffee. I didn't know what to expect. Maybe he would make excuses or point an accusing finger of blame at me for our broken relationship. My fears, however, were unfounded. Dad simply said he was sorry and asked me to forgive him and let him have the opportunity to be part of my life. I went into our meeting estranged from my father, but I came out of it in a cautious but joyful reconciliation that never wavered from that day on.

As much as separation from an earthly father can impact our life, it pales in comparison to the consequences of being estranged from our heavenly Father. Unlike weak human relationships, our separation from God is not part his fault and part ours; it is totally due to our sin. God's love for us is so intense and full of grace that he sent his perfect Son, Jesus, to bear our past, present, and future sins on the cross. When we trust Jesus and place our faith in him, we acknowledge this great gift and become righteous in God's eyes. He sees us as holy where we had been sinful; he sees us as blameless where we had been guilty; he sees us in a new and sacred position, reconciled to the God we once rejected.

Heavenly Father,
I thank you that you are the God of reconciliation.
What wonderful news! Incredibly, you have made
flawed believers the ambassadors of this message.
Although the sin that caused my separation from you
was totally my responsibility, the means to removing
it was totally your work through Jesus Christ.
Thank you, God. In Jesus' name. Amen.

Psalm for the Soul
The LORD is gracious and righteous;
our God is full of compassion. (Ps. 116:5)

Divine Diagnosis

*On hearing this, Jesus said, "It is not the healthy
who need a doctor, but the sick."*
MATTHEW 9:12

There is an art to diagnosis. Outward signs may suggest many different ailments, but a skilled physician can rule out the imitators and find the true cause. Once the diagnosis has been correctly made, help for the symptoms, or even a cure, may be possible.

Jesus was the Master of the diagnosis of sin-sickness. He was able to look at the outward life and see into the ailing spirit. Many times Jesus mercifully healed the sick, the blind, the mute, and he even raised the dead. These actions teach us that God is compassionate and merciful when we suffer and able to perfectly heal that which he created. Even more astonishing, however, is his ability to detect, diagnose, and cure hidden sin. He sees both the obvious and the subtle symptoms of a life separated from God.

Generally, self-diagnosis is a dangerous thing when it comes to the care of our bodies, but it is an essential element when assessing our spiritual health. The Pharisees relied on outward rituals and sacrifices thinking they would secure their spiritual position, but the Lord cares nothing about empty formalities. Unlike the "sinners" who knew they were sick and in need of a Doctor, the Pharisees were in a much more perilous position: they were eternally terminal and didn't know it.

You may be deep in the throes of complex medical problems and treatment, but what would Jesus diagnose about the condition of your soul? A soul sick with sin and separation from God is the most serious and deadly disease one can have. Jesus' specialty is the soul, and he is the only sovereign, merciful Physician who can heal it. Only you and the Lord know if you are sick with unrepented and unforgiven sin. The closer you come to the end of this life, the more dangerous and deadly your condition becomes. Are you fixated on physical health at the expense of your eternal well-being, or have you entrusted the care of both body and soul to the Lord?

If you haven't already, today is the day to seek the Great Physician and the healing only he can offer. When you seek him in earnest humility, you will find him. His cure is thorough, complete, compassionate, and eternal. Tell him you know you are sick with sin and you need his healing forgiveness. Pray that he will forgive you and save your soul for eternity. What could you possibly have to lose?

> *Dear Lord,*
> *I am physically sick, and I fear that my eternal soul*
> *may be sick, too. You have told me that if I confess*
> *my sins you will forgive me and cleanse me from all*
> *unrighteousness. I want to be new, clean, and healthily*
> *restored to the depths of my soul. Thank you for taking*
> *the punishment that was meant for me when you died*
> *on the cross. Thank you for offering me life, peace, and*
> *joy with you in heaven. I accept your incredible sacrifice*
> *and give you what's left of my earthly life and my soul*
> *for eternity. Amen.*

Psalm for the Soul

Blessed is he whose
transgressions are forgiven,
whose sins are covered. (Ps. 32:1)

The Call of Faith

Is any one of you sick? He should call the elders of the church to pray over him and anoint him with oil in the name of the Lord.
JAMES 5:14

*I*n my own experience with becoming suddenly and seriously ill, I ran the gamut of emotions. One of the predominate feelings was that of utter helplessness. In this passage, however, James sees things differently. He tells us that there are definite actions we can take when we find ourselves facing a grave sickness; we can call for the elders of the church to pray over us. It may sound like a simple act, but sometimes it's deceptively difficult to ask for the help we need.

Some people may even think that they shouldn't have to inform the elders of their condition, believing it's their duty to know about it and offer to come pray for them. But I don't think it's an accident that this passage lays the responsibility of asking for prayer at the feet of the one who is ill. Initiating this process is a clear act of faith. In placing that call, we demonstrate our confidence that, while God's ways are not our own, we will nonetheless trust and obey.

I've had two personal experiences with James 5:14. The first came years ago when my mom was diagnosed with cancer. I flew to Denver to be with her for her surgery. We spent the days prior to her hospitalization searching the Word for guidance and hope, when the Lord brought this passage to our attention. Mom was not closely connected with a church fellowship at the time, so we called the elders of my church long distance and arranged for them to pray at a specific time while I anointed Mom with oil. She did not have an instantaneous healing, but the years would bear witness to the fact that she outlived the most optimistic estimation the doctors could give.

The second experience was recently after I was diagnosed with acute leukemia. I asked the elders to come pray for me while I was home for a while between hospitalizations. I'll admit that during the time they prayed and afterward, I did not feel a supernatural sensation of healing. Although they prayed that I would be healed, the greater emphasis was on the desire that God would be glorified in my illness regardless of whether I was cured.

How like our Lord to shine light on the first step we should take when we are confused and overwhelmed with sickness. If you are ill, call your church and ask the elders to pray for you according to James 5:14. If you are too sick to call, ask someone to call for you. You may be healed or you may not be healed, but you have shown that you trust God with your very life.

> *Father God,*
> *Thank you for this Scripture that gives a pattern of action*
> *to take when I am dealing with the chaos of illness.*
> *In this greatly humbling time, if I have unconfessed sin*
> *in my life, shine your light on it so that I will eagerly*
> *confess it to you now. I ask for forgiveness; I ask for*
> *healing; but mostly I ask that my heart is right with*
> *you and that you will be glorified no matter what.*
> *In Jesus' name. Amen.*

Psalm for the Soul

The LORD will sustain him on his sickbed
and restore him from his bed of illness. (Ps. 41:3)

Wondering Why

And Joshua said, "Ah, Sovereign LORD, why did you
ever bring this people across the Jordan to deliver
us into the hands of the Amorites to destroy us?"
JOSHUA 7:7

*I*t is human nature to want to understand the reason we are
going through trials and troubles. However, sometimes we
Christians hide our true questions out of fear that we may
step over the line and offend God. But there is a difference between
not trusting God and not understanding his ways. Even Joshua,
who walked closely with God, still asked "why?" when his military
met with sudden defeat.

Under Joshua's leadership Israel had experienced an amazing
victory culminating with the wall of Jericho falling and the city
being taken by the Israelites. Clearly, God was on the side of Israel.
They must have felt invincible. So it was all the more shocking
when the next battle, that looked to be an easy victory, resulted in
a sound defeat. Joshua was baffled. He worried about the repercussions on Israel's future, and, more importantly, he worried
about the impact of a humiliating loss on the "great name" of God.

Joshua had been mentored by Moses and talked directly to
God, but even so, on the heels of this defeat, he grappled with
many of the same questions we struggle with today. He reassessed
his past actions looking for clues: "If only we had been content to
stay on the other side of the Jordan!" (v. 7). Most of us have made
the same kind of "if only" statement at one time or another, but
Joshua's momentary regret is all the more amazing in view of the
fact that God had parted the Jordan River so that Joshua and his
people could cross on dry ground!

To some, Joshua's questioning might have been interpreted
as insolent, but God saw his heart and knew that he wasn't filled
with pity or self-interest but with concern for Israel and for God's

reputation. He wanted to please God above all else and was honestly wrestling to reconcile his defeat in view of what he understood as God's will.

Even though puzzled, he addressed God as "Sovereign Lord," which indicated his belief and respect. In that sovereignty, Joshua understood that God was not ruled by any outside circumstance but was Lord of all: timing, events, victories and defeats, life and death.

We, too, can be honest about the questions we have regarding our own lives. We can ask God to reveal his purpose in events that are not our will but may indeed be his. Like Joshua, if we love God and our goal is to glorify him, we can ask the questions on our heart. He may answer our request and allow us to understand, and, then again, he may not. Either way we trust him; either way he is our God.

Father God,
You are sovereign and under no obligation to inform me
of your ways. You know my thoughts anyway, so I will
ask the honest questions that I have withheld out of fear
of being insulting or seeming to doubt you. I may not
understand why, but I release the private doubts that
have kept me from drawing near to you.
In Jesus' name. Amen.

Psalm for the Soul

I say to God my Rock,
"Why have you forgotten me?
Why must I go about mourning,
oppressed by the enemy?" (Ps. 42:9)

The Power of Weakness

*But he said to me, "My grace is sufficient for you,
for my power is made perfect in weakness."*
2 CORINTHIANS 12:9

*I*llness brings with it a host of humbling losses. Among those losses, one of the most difficult to accept is the loss of physical strength. Weakness impacts everything we do and everything we consider doing. It changes our perception of ourselves, and, because weakness is often observable, it can also change the way we are treated by others. In an achievement-oriented culture such as ours, weakness is a dreaded and terrible thing.

Yet the Apostle Paul had the audacity to boast of his own weakness and regard it as a blessing. Paul's life and achievements would not have suggested a weak life. His lineage, upbringing, and training had placed him at the pinnacle of power in his society. Before the Lord confronted him on the road to Damascus, Paul was using this authority and strength to persecute and kill Christians. We also know that after his conversion, God privileged him with a view of heaven that was so wondrous he was not permitted to speak of it. His was not the profile of a weakling.

Paul did, however, know something of weakness. The Lord had given him a physical ailment, a "thorn in the flesh" to offset the pride of having been given such extraordinary insight into paradise. Paul prayed three times that God would see fit to remove his ailment, but God denied his requests. Why, then, did Paul go from praying that God would remove his "thorn" to boasting about his suffering and weakness? What had he learned about suffering?

The Lord knows that suffering and weakness provide the best avenue for power to be observed and demonstrated. Like a master artist, the Lord chooses the individual whose humbling circumstances have made him a blank canvas that will not compete with the clear presentation of the power of his message. When we have pridefully scribbled our accomplishments across our lives, that's all others can see, so we have limited our usefulness to God. But when we are weak and willing, no one can possibly credit the masterpiece for the common and utilitarian canvas it's painted upon.

Isn't it like our creative and compassionate God to use us when we feel the least up to the task? To those around us who understand our condition, our economy of words suddenly carry more weight and, because our energy is in short supply, our actions are more meaningful.

Rather than hopelessly mourning the loss of strength, offer yourself to God. Ask him to create a lasting masterpiece across the canvas of your diminishing life and health.

Father God,
You are well acquainted with the power of weakness.
After all, you came to us from heaven in the form of a
helpless baby, born humbly to a poor mother. You lived
your life as a servant and died an ignoble death. Yet you
are pure power and pure love. Lord, take my failing
health and the limitations of my life and, by your grace,
use it for others to see your glory. Amen.

Psalm for the Soul

My soul will boast in the LORD;
let the afflicted hear and rejoice. (Ps. 34:2)

Help for Unbelief

Immediately the boy's father cried out and said,
"I do believe; help my unbelief."
Mark 9:24 NASB

For years this poor father had watched helplessly as his son was overwhelmed with convulsions. The boy was unable to speak; and in the throes of an attack, he foamed at the mouth, gnashed his teeth, and became deathly rigid. There were times when the fit propelled him into the water where he could have drowned or into a fire where he might have been burned.

Finally, in desperation, the man had come to the disciples and asked them to drive out the evil spirit that had control of his son. But despite their efforts they were unable to do it. And then Jesus came on the scene. The father wasted no time explaining the situation to him.

"Bring the boy to me," Jesus said.

When the evil spirit saw Jesus, he threw the boy into a massive convulsion, as though he knew his time of controlling this young man was running out. The father said to Jesus, "But if you can do anything, take pity on us and help us" (v. 22).

"'If you can'?" said Jesus, "Everything is possible for him who believes" (v. 23).

I can almost hear the heart-wrenching cry of the father as he answered, "I do believe; help my unbelief."

It's so easy to identify with the internal war of belief and unbelief this man was experiencing. Haven't we all been exhausted and worn down by a persistent problem that has played out over and over before our eyes? Haven't we felt our beliefs run into the brick wall of faltering faith? Yet even at this crossroads of doubt and faith, the man looked to Jesus to supply the power he needed to come to him in total reliance. It wasn't a problem of a lack of power on God's part; it was a matter of the necessary faith on the part of the father.

What doctors, healers, and even the disciples had been unable to accomplish, Jesus did with a calm command: "'You deaf and mute spirit,' he said, 'I command you, come out of him and never enter him again'" (v. 25).

In our weakness we can go to God. Even though we have no ability to strengthen our own faith, our plea for greater faith, like the plea of the desperate father, is an act of faith in itself. "Bring the boy to me," Jesus said. That's the first step of faith. Bring your cares to Jesus, and ask him to help you with any lingering unbelief.

> *Holy Father,*
> *I know I don't have a solid grasp on your power and*
> *your willingness to move mountains when I show a*
> *mustard seed of faith. Let me learn from this loving*
> *father who approached you not in obstinate refusal to*
> *believe but from a struggle of belief and doubt that*
> *can douse the flame of faith. Let me just as surely*
> *cry out to you with my cares, my long-held problems,*
> *my chronic pain, my "impossible situation,"*
> *and say to you, "I do believe; help my unbelief."*
> *In Jesus' name. Amen.*

Psalm for the Soul

Hear, O LORD, and be merciful to me;
O LORD, be my help. (Ps. 30:10)

The Sin Solution

Peter replied, "Repent and be baptized, every one of you,
in the name of Jesus Christ for the forgiveness of your sins."
ACTS 2:38

*A*t some unknown, silent moment, a single cell in my blood began to grow uncontrollably. Although outwardly I continued to go through my usual routine, my true condition was far from normal. I was in great peril. It wasn't until my blood was drawn and unflinchingly analyzed by the doctor that I was confronted with the truth of my condition. At that point I had two choices: I could squarely face the existence of my illness and follow the doctor's regimen of treatment, or I could passively ignore the existence of this deadly cancer and die.

In the book of Acts, we see Peter as the divinely appointed "doctor" who confronted the men of Israel with the cancer of their sin. Filled with the Holy Spirit, Peter laid out the facts of their behavior toward Jesus: "This man was handed over to you by God's set purpose and foreknowledge; and you, with the help of wicked men, put him to death by nailing him to the cross" (2:23).

He then went on to remind them of the prophecies from the Old Testament that foretold of the coming of Jesus through the line of David. These men, who had been raised in expectation of the coming Messiah, had not only failed to recognize him; they had crucified him! Upon hearing the truth and recognizing their sin, the people "were cut to the heart and said to Peter and the other apostles, 'Brothers, what shall we do?'" (v. 37). They had to make a choice. Either they could ignore their horrendous sin and its consequence of death and separation from Christ for eternity, or they could repent and seek God's forgiveness.

The dilemma is the same for each one of us. What *shall* we do with the problem of our sin? We may not have been there to hoist the cross on Jesus' shoulder, but every time we defiantly defend our wrong behavior, we are essentially poising the spike over Jesus' wrist. Each time we deny the God who loves us and selfishly choose our own interests over the will of God, we are flaunting our sin before the Savior who died in our place.

Thankfully, Peter not only presented them with the evidence of their sin; he showed them the way to the cure for it as well. "Repent and be baptized, every one of you, in the name of Jesus Christ for the forgiveness of your sins" (v. 38).

The solution to the sin problem remains true to this day. Don't leave the cancer of sin untreated and find yourself forever separated from the Savior. Confess your sin and call on Christ to forgive you. He will. And when you leave this world, you will enter vibrant joy and life with Jesus.

Father God,
Enable me to see my sin for what it is: a dark and
multiplying cancer that will rob me of life and eternity
with you. I'm sorry for my sin, and through the power
of the Holy Spirit, I turn away from it right now.
Thank you for dying for me so that I might be with
you forever. In Jesus' name. Amen.

Psalm for the Soul

Then I acknowledged my sin to you
and did not cover up my iniquity.
I said, "I will confess
my transgressions to the Lord"—
and you forgave
the guilt of my sin. (Ps. 32:5)

Dealing with Doubts

*"Unless I see the nail marks in his hands and put
my finger where the nails were, and put my hand
into his side, I will not believe it."*
JOHN 20:25

ecause of this statement, Thomas earned the dubious honor
of being referred to throughout history as "doubting
Thomas." But I believe it's too easy to think of Thomas simply as the only disciple whose faith was so weak that he needed
hard evidence before he would believe that Christ had risen from
the dead. Perhaps he was a thoughtful and serious person, skeptical of things out of the ordinary and careful before pledging his
allegiance to anyone. And maybe we are just a little bit like him.

We know that Thomas felt a deep allegiance to the Lord. When
Jesus announced he was going to Bethany after Lazarus' death,
Thomas fully expected that the Jews would find them and kill Jesus
and the disciples. Yet he was prepared to go and resigned to die if
necessary—a decision that reflected his intense loyalty and love for
the Lord.

Later, when Jesus was preparing his disciples for his death on
the cross, Thomas asked the Lord to explain what he meant. The
others probably wanted to ask but were unwilling to risk looking
foolish. Thomas, however, was not content to *pretend* he understood; he wanted a genuine grasp of what the Lord had said.

Then, the unthinkable. Jesus was brought up on bogus charges
and sentenced to the most horrendous and humiliating death possible: crucifixion. The disciples were heartbroken and fearful for their
own safety. They all huddled together behind locked doors—all but
Thomas. When the Lord miraculously entered the locked room and
showed them the scars on his hands and his side, Thomas was not
there to see. Was he mourning in seclusion? Had he vowed never
again to allow himself to be vulnerable and believing? Now that

Jesus was dead, was he wondering how he would face his family, his friends, his future? Had the last three years of his life been wasted?

We don't know his thoughts. But when the disciples told him they had seen the risen Jesus, Thomas was not about to accept it blindly: "Unless I see the nail marks in his hands and put my finger where the nails were, and put my hand into his side, I will not believe it."

A week later Jesus once again appeared to the disciples and to Thomas. Jesus turned to him and said, "Put your finger here; see my hands. Reach out your hand and put it into my side. Stop doubting and believe" (v. 27).

Nothing in the Bible indicates that Thomas found it necessary to actually touch the scars. I suspect that the magnificent sight of the glorified Lord was evidence enough. Did Thomas bow his head in shame for his willful unbelief? Did he fall to his knees? All we know is that all his doubt shattered in the brilliance of pure truth, and Thomas touchingly declared his worship and his belief when he said, "My Lord and my God!" (v. 28).

Dear Father in heaven,
Like Thomas, there have been times when I have
deliberately decided that I will not believe. Forgive me,
Lord, and give me the faith to make the willing choice
to "stop doubting and believe." You have said that those
who believe without seeing are blessed. Bless me now,
and erase any lingering doubt. Thank you, my Lord
and my God! Amen.

Psalm for the Soul
But I trust in you, O LORD;
I say, "You are my God." (Ps. 31:14)

Casting Lessons

Cast all your anxiety on him because he cares for you.
1 PETER 5:7

W hen I was young, Dad sometimes took me fishing. As I stood beside him on the bank of the stream, he would thoughtfully "read" the water: "There's a nice little pocket over there where the bank's been undercut by the current." After more study, he might say, "Downstream a ways there's a riffle. Old Mr. Trout just loves those sunny shallows."

Then, in hip waders and hat, with his fishing rod held to the side, he stepped through the rushing water and over the rocks until he steadied himself at the desired spot in the streambed. He was partial to the swirling eddies that formed behind a boulder or a tree fallen across the water. With the target solidly in sight, he brought the rod behind him and flicked it out before him like a bullwhip. The reel hummed as the line sailed through the air. Once the fly had settled, he pulled the weblike line until it fell in a cascade before him and then began slowly winding it back onto the reel.

As far as I was concerned, catching the fish was not nearly as interesting as the systematic approach to finding them and the dance of casting the line. Dad could fish for hours. His patience and faith seemed inexhaustible. Although he couldn't see what was happening below the water's surface, he trusted that the well-placed fly was doing its job and would eventually yield the reward of a fine rainbow trout.

Under the burden of illness, pain, and worry, the casting of our cares upon the Lord can be a much more haphazard process than the thoughtful casting of a fisherman's line. Rather than a confident placement of our troubles that comes from a studied faith in the character of God, our efforts more often seem like a feeble toss of a heavenward prayer—one that seems to plop right back into our own palm. Maybe we wonder if our problems are just too big for God. But the intensity of our trial does not diminish his power any more than his love for us is diminished by our puny faith. When we cast our cares and fears upon him, we aim at a mighty target: the cross of Jesus. There our sins have been paid for, the battle fought, the ultimate victory won.

Like the dedicated angler, we can regard life's rapids, slippery rocks, and icy waters as inevitable obstacles that will not prevent us from focusing on Christ. And, while waiting for the answer to our prayer, we can recall the steady faith of the fisherman and know that Jesus is just outside of our field of vision working things together for our good.

Father God,
I know that I can't cast my cares upon you without
keeping you always before me. My own failings burden
me with the troubles you never wanted me to carry.
Teach me to precisely aim my heart and my cares
at the Savior. And then, Lord, help me to let
them go. Amen.

Psalm for the Soul

Cast your cares on the LORD
and he will sustain you;
he will never let the righteous fall. (Ps. 55:22)

Sweet Sorrow

*For you became sorrowful as God intended and so were
not harmed in any way by us. Godly sorrow brings
repentance that leads to salvation and leaves no regret,
but worldly sorrow brings death.*
2 CORINTHIANS 7:9–10

No one wants to reach the end of life only to look back and
feel sorrow and regret. The sadness may be there because
loved ones have already died and left a painful void, or
other important relationships may have gradually eroded or disappeared entirely. Certainly sorrow comes from missed opportunities
and the loss of youth and health. All of these things are understandable reasons for sorrow. Excessive sorrow, however, can be
consuming and destructive. When we are overwhelmed with
despair, remorse, or bitterness about the disappointments of life,
sorrow can spiral out of control and defeat us.

Having said that, the surprising truth is that not all sorrow is
bad. A good sorrow, a godly sorrow, brings an individual to salvation, peace, and victory. It is what the Apostle Paul is speaking of
in this passage: the sorrow that leads to repentance.

I experienced this kind of sorrow years ago when I was becoming aware of my own need for a Savior. My children were young,
and I worried about them growing up in a mean and unreliable
world. I could somewhat protect them now, but what about later
through the chances and changes of growing up? Was there no certainty that I could count on? In my curiosity and need, I began
reading books about Jesus and listening to Christian teaching. As
I became more aware of God's standard of holiness, it became
apparent that I had missed the mark. In view of this discovery,
there was no way to explain my feelings other than to say
I felt a deep sorrow. Yet that painful sorrow led to a wonderful
result. I began to understand that in going my own way through

life, I had been rebelling against my Creator. Eventually I repented, sought forgiveness, and asked Jesus to come into my heart and be Lord of my life. God miraculously answered that prayer! At that moment my life here on earth and my eternity were forever changed.

Although God's standards never vary, he graciously deals with us in our unique individuality. Almost without fail, we see our need for him in light of the sorrow of realizing our own efforts have fallen pitifully short of his standards. If you are feeling this sorrow now, welcome it and follow the leading to agree with God that you are a sinner who needs a Savior. Thank God for the sweet sorrow that drives you to his arms.

> Lord God,
> *There is no hiding when you shine your spotlight*
> *on my heart and reveal my inadequacy to rule my own*
> *life. I have sinned; I have rebelled; and the sorrows*
> *from these actions are now driving me to you. Help me*
> *find the courage to face the truth and ask for forgiveness*
> *so that I can enter into the joy of my Lord.*
> *In Jesus' name. Amen.*

Psalm for the Soul

The cords of death entangled me,
the anguish of the grave came upon me;
I was overcome by trouble and sorrow.
Then I called on the name of the LORD:
"O LORD, save me!" (Ps. 116:3–4)

Passing Pilgrims

Dear friends, I urge you, as aliens and strangers in the world,
to abstain from sinful desires, which war against your soul.
Live such good lives among the pagans that, though they
accuse you of doing wrong, they may see your good deeds
and glorify God on the day he visits us.
1 PETER 2:11–12

*I*f you have ever traveled outside the country, you know the feeling of being a stranger. The language may be different, the customs unfamiliar, and the style of dress unlike anything you have ever worn. Chances are that the local people of this country will figure out rather quickly that you are not one of them. Maybe it's the camera hanging from your neck, your white tennis shoes, or the guidebook and dictionary you consult on a regular basis. But while you are trying to understand their culture, you can bet that they are looking at you as a representative of your country. Your behavior, whether dignified and respectful or critical and judgmental, will be a strong basis for their opinion about your country.

As believers in Jesus, we experience a similar scrutiny. At the moment we received Jesus as our Savior, our citizenship changed. We may still live in the same house in the same city, but our home country leaped the borders of this earth and became heaven. People who have known us for years may begin to look at us with curious interest. Something's different, but they can't quite put their finger on it.

Our behavior is often the clue that tips off the fact that we are Christians. In this passage Peter cautions us to live such good lives that even when others are looking for ways to discredit us, all they will find are lives that glorify God. Rather than being individuals who cause dissension and behave in rowdy disobedience, we are peacemakers and truth seekers. Rather than harboring grudges against fellow believers, we love them out of reverence for our God. Rather than providing fuel for foolish and defaming talk from unbelievers, our exemplary behavior silences criticism.

As anyone who has experienced life in a foreign land will tell you, it is difficult to be far from home. We long for the ease and familiarity of our life. Oddly, Christians often feel like strangers in the world even when in our native land. Our true citizenship is in heaven, and there is a sense of longing for the rights and privileges that are reserved for its own.

Until the Lord takes us to heaven, it's wise to remember that we are only passing pilgrims compelled to live in a place that is not our permanent home. We may not be able to picture our heavenly country, but when we get there, we will be strangers no more. We will be full citizens with full rights; we will be home.

Heavenly Father,
I do feel like a stranger here on earth at times.
Let me lead my life in such a way that I honor
your great name. Amen.

Psalm for the Soul

Hear my prayer, O LORD,
listen to my cry for help;
be not deaf to my weeping.
For I dwell with you as an alien,
a stranger, as all my fathers were. (Ps. 39:12)

The Focus Factor

*Therefore we do not lose heart. Though outwardly we are
wasting away, yet inwardly we are being renewed day by day.
For our light and momentary troubles are achieving for us an
eternal glory that far outweighs them all. So we fix our eyes
not on what is seen, but on what is unseen. For what is seen
is temporary, but what is unseen is eternal.*

2 Corinthians 4:16–18

*I*f we didn't know who had written these verses, we would
be inclined to think that this individual had never been
acquainted with real pain and suffering. We might assume
he was one of those rare and lucky individuals who had somehow
escaped the losses and tragedies that most of us endure. After all,
he called his troubles "light and momentary"; few of us would
characterize our problems in that way.

Paul the apostle wrote this. His life dramatically changed when
Jesus confronted him on the Damascus road, and since that time,
his existence had been far from tranquil. Drama and danger characterized his life, and a close look at Paul, the man, would have
revealed a back scarred with 195 stripes from five lashings by the
Jews. He was beaten with rods, stoned, and left for dead. He had
been shipwrecked three times and endured the insults of natural
disasters and random crime. Persecuted by his adversaries and
betrayed by trusted but false brothers, he had also known hunger
and thirst, cold and nakedness. He had been exhausted yet sleep-
less and carried the heartfelt concern and responsibility for the
fledgling churches (see 2 Cor. 11:24–29).

After all that, the apostle still referred to his troubles as "light
and momentary"! Either Paul was a person who could not face
reality, or he had a different understanding of the role his earthly
troubles played in the bigger picture of his eternal life.

If his concentration were fixed solely on his afflictions, he would have been a miserable man. No one needed to remind Paul that our bodies are perishing instruments that serve us only for this short time on earth. Yet rather than mourning fading youth and the wasting away of strength, Paul focused on his inner man where the radiant, replenishing love of Christ resided. Although the inevitable processes of aging and death were at work in his body, he was being renewed spiritually day by day as he grew in grace and understanding. Only on the outside was there decay and death; on the inside was vitality and life eternal.

Paul held up this present life in continual comparison to the unseen life of glory that was to come. As a result, his trials served to wean him from dependence on the world and its passing troubles, and, instead, sharpened his concentration on the coming glory of heaven.

Even when chaos swirls around us and trials rise before us, we can strive to bring all these factors into the focus of being, first and foremost, a child of God. Our troubles *are* temporary, but our joy in Jesus will last forever.

Father God,
There is a grim reality to illness and the wearing out
of my earthly body. It seems that I am constantly reminded
of my losses. Break my concentration on these earthly matters,
and let me see only you with the eyes of my heart. Amen.

Psalm for the Soul

You guide me with your counsel,
and afterward you will take me into glory. (Ps. 73:24)

The Source of Wisdom

*If any of you lacks wisdom, he should ask God, who gives gener-
ously to all without finding fault, and it will be given to him.*
JAMES 1:5

I
f ever wisdom is needed, it is when we are making the hard
decisions that come at the end of life. At a time when we
pictured life mellowing out and becoming simpler, it seems
that everywhere we turn is a new and daunting trial. We somehow
thought the golden years were supposed to be carefree, but now
we wonder if they're called *golden* years because that's what we
need—more gold!

For instance, even if we've had relatively good health all our
lives, now we may face new realities of illness and pain. We had
hoped our finances would last through our lifetime, but the costs
of living in addition to medical and other forms of care are
shockingly high. Then there are the complicated decisions on
such tedious matters as wills, trusts, powers of attorney, advance
health-care directives, and executors. These are serious decisions
that require good information and good counsel, but mostly they
require wisdom.

Take heart. One of the great assurances we have from our Lord
is the promise that he will give us wisdom when we ask for it. He
gives generously and without the condemning and dreaded "I told
you so!" Not surprisingly, the way the Lord cultivates wisdom in
us is by allowing trials in our lives that have the potential of pro-
ducing greater dependence on him and subsequently strengthening
our faith.

If this is discouraging, keep in mind that you have probably
already been struggling with these trials for a while. However,
it may be clearer and clearer that you need God's help to get
through them. How wonderful! This is solid evidence that God is

answering your prayers for wisdom because seeking God's will and power is always a wise thing to do.

Through the process of prayerful deliberation, you may see other subtle benefits such as trusting God more consistently and resisting your old impulse to doubt. These beautiful rewards are gradually maturing and strengthening your faith. The Lord lets us know that while wisdom is available to us free for the asking, it is never cheap.

Lord,
Give me wisdom and your guidance as I face difficult
decisions. I feel pressured and intimidated as I struggle
to understand complicated terms and concepts. Drive
away my doubt and let my eyes, heart, and mind rest
clearly on you. Amen.

Psalm for the Soul

Surely you desire truth in the inner parts;
you teach me wisdom in the inmost place. (Ps. 51:6)

If Only . . .

"Lord," Martha said to Jesus, "if you had been here,
my brother would not have died. But I know that even
now God will give you whatever you ask."
JOHN 11:21–22

*W*hat a temptation to look back on past events with regret. It's easy to become stuck in a maddening quagmire of wondering what would have happened if things had been different. Maybe if we'd seen another doctor, or gotten medical help at the first sign of symptoms, or taken better care of ourselves, we wouldn't be wrestling with illness now.

When Lazarus died, his sisters, Martha and Mary, couldn't help wondering what would have happened if Jesus had been there when he fell sick. In this passage of Scripture, we have a window into the heart and mind of Martha as she struggled to understand her brother's death and why God allowed it.

To help us step into her shoes, let's take a few liberties and imagine what she might have written about those events:

- Day 1: Lazarus has taken ill. We have sent word to Jesus because we know he loves us and will come to heal our brother. I pray he comes quickly.
- Day 2: Our dear brother has died. We wrapped him in grave cloths and placed him in a tomb. We can't stop weeping. Mary can scarcely move, so great is her grief. Jesus still has not come. I don't understand why.
- Day 4: It's been four days since we buried Lazarus. When I heard that Jesus was on his way from Jerusalem, I went to the edge of town to meet him. I told him that if only he had been here, Lazarus wouldn't have died. Jesus answered that my brother would rise again. I said, "I know he will rise again in the resurrection at the last day" (v. 24).

Then Jesus said the most astonishing thing: "I am the resurrection and the life. He who believes in me will live, even though he dies; and whoever lives and believes in me will never die." Then he looked right into my eyes and asked, "Do you believe this?' (vv. 25–26).

I knew deep in my spirit that he was the Messiah we had waited for, so I answered, "I believe that you are the Christ, the Son of God, who was to come into the world" (v. 27).

A while later, Mary and I and many others were there when Jesus had the stone rolled away from the tomb. I was concerned because after four days the body would have begun to decay. But Jesus reminded me to believe and said I would see the glory of God. Then he called, "Lazarus, come out!" (v. 43).

I held my breath as our dear brother emerged from the tomb still wrapped in strips of linen with the burial cloth around his face! What joy! But in the midst of the celebration, I could only ponder Jesus. This Man is more than a healer; he holds the power over life and death. He is more than a prophet because he not only sees the future; he controls it. This Jesus, he is God!

Holy Father,
Encourage me to trust you in the midst of circumstances
that seem haphazard or accidental. Like Martha,
I am inclined to tell you how to work in the
ways I think are best. But you are God, and you,
not I, are in control. Let me remember that you
love me with the same powerful love with which you
loved Martha, Mary, and Lazarus. Amen.

Psalm for the Soul
The LORD is righteous in all his ways
and loving toward all he has made. (Ps. 145:17)

Temporary Temples

Do you not know that your body is a temple of the Holy Spirit, who is in you, whom you have received from God? You are not your own; you were bought at a price. Therefore honor God with your body.

1 CORINTHIANS 6:19–20

*I*n 1940, during the blitz of World War II, German planes relentlessly firebombed London. Located in the heart of the city is St. Paul's Cathedral, a masterpiece of architecture designed by Sir Christopher Wren and built over a thirty-five-year period from 1675 to 1710. During the year and a half of bombings, while most of the surrounding area was destroyed, the cathedral sustained only moderate damage to the basic structure. At one point a bomb landed directly in the nave but miraculously failed to detonate. The image of the magnificent dome of St. Paul's Cathedral, wreathed in flames and smoke, became a symbol of steadfast hope, survival, and the presence of God to the war-weary Londoners.

A grand cathedral like St. Paul's seems to capture our respect, but even when the structure is a modest church, we hold reverential feelings about our places of worship. We are inclined to think that within their walls God manifests his presence. We spend vast amounts of money and time creating churches in the hope that they will do justice to our perception of God.

But God looks past structures of brick and mortar and, incredibly, considers our frail and perishable bodies as the ideal temples for his own Holy Spirit to reside. There he is truly manifested and able to make his presence known to believers and unbelievers alike. Whether we are young and brimming with vitality to do the Lord's work or struggling in an ill and aging body, we must regard these fragile structures with the same respect we would show a lovely church or cathedral.

The most serious damage to St. Paul's sustained in the bombings was the total destruction of the interior high altar. In contrast, the outer structure of our bodies will ultimately deteriorate, but the high altar of our soul is forever vibrant with eternal and indestructible life.

Heavenly Father,
You are the Master Architect of this frail temple of
a body. Let me honor you by submitting my will, my
body, and my soul to you and your purposes. Whether
in this life or in the life to come, I am yours—
purchased at the price of your precious blood to do
with me as you please. Amen.

Psalm for the Soul

I will praise you, O LORD, with all my heart;
before the "gods" I will sing your praise.
I will bow down toward your holy temple
and will praise your name
and your love and your faithfulness,
for you have exalted above all things
your name and your word. (Ps. 138:1–2)

Less Is More

"He must become greater; I must become less."
JOHN 3:30

When heavyweight boxing champ Mohammad Ali arrogantly announced to the world, "I am the greatest!" it was a stunning display of unabashed pride. There was no arguing that he was a great boxer, but his own assessment of his abilities left little room for praise from anyone else. Yet rather than being turned off by his show of pride, people were fascinated. I believe his statement dignified a secret mind-set of many people who really feel that *they* are the most important, the best, and—well—the greatest.

In contrast to such arrogance, John the Baptist saw his purpose in life solely in the subservient position of pointing sinners to the One who was truly great: the Messiah, Jesus Christ. John himself was an exceptional man from extraordinary beginnings. When his mother, Elizabeth, was carrying him, none other than the angel Gabriel came to announce his impending birth to John's father. Gabriel characterized the yet-unborn John by saying, "He will be great in the sight of the Lord" (Luke 1:15). As if that were not cause enough for pride, the Lord Jesus said of John: "Among those born of women there has not risen anyone greater than John the Baptist" (Matt. 11:11). In spite of being called "great" by an angel and by Jesus, John saw his place in utter deference to his Lord, saying, "He must become greater; I must become less." It was, in fact, his humility that made him great.

Such humility does not come naturally to man, especially when in the prime of vigor and life. As age and infirmity set in, we become more aware that any strength or greatness we might have once possessed is fleeting. Even Ali's strength and ability were eventually defeated as he faced aging and disease.

Rather than viewing humility as a substandard condition, John the Baptist saw it as the only appropriate response to a Holy God. He loved his role of preparing the way for the Lord, and he hated it when men attempted to compare him to Jesus. Even when John was in his mother's womb, he supernaturally recognized Jesus as God. When Mary and Elizabeth saw each other for the first time since they were both expecting, Scripture tells us that Elizabeth said to Mary, "But why am I so favored that the mother of my Lord would come to me? As soon as the sound of your greeting reached my ears, the baby in my womb leaped for joy" (Luke 1:43–44).

As believers we have the unique inclination to inwardly leap for joy out of love for Jesus even though physically we are day by day "becoming less" due to age or failing health. Incredibly, we have a Savior who has prepared the way to the future for us by laying down his life so that we might live forever with him. Until we are in his presence, we still have the opportunity and privilege of pointing others to the "Greatest": Jesus Christ.

Heavenly Father,
Like John, I want to willingly take the backseat and
point others to you. Help me strive to be content only
when I have allowed the Lord to become greater and
greater in my own life. In Jesus' name. Amen.

Psalm for the Soul

You save the humble
but bring low those whose
eyes are haughty. (Ps. 18:27)

The View from the Waiting Room

Not only so, but we ourselves, who have the firstfruits
of the Spirit, groan inwardly as we wait eagerly for
our adoption as sons, the redemption of our bodies.
For in this hope we were saved.
ROMANS 8:23–24

Anyone who has been seriously ill is well acquainted with waiting rooms. No matter which doctor's office or hospital we are in, all waiting rooms have a similar atmosphere. Time seems to stand still when you're waiting. You can look at the clock and see that it's 1:30, then in what seems like an hour, you look again to find that it is only 1:40. Magazines should help pass the time, but the only ones on the table are from 1997, and they have names like *Computer Diagnostics* and *Popular Paperclips*.

Waiting is tough. When we wait, we are usually in one of two modes: dread or anticipation. This is never so true as when we consider waiting for the return of the Lord and pondering eternal life. We may not be able to picture exactly what we are waiting for, but through the Holy Spirit we have a taste and an eager anticipation for the glory that is to come. Therefore, we yearn for a redeemed body that is not destined for death. As believers, our souls are already redeemed and ready for eternity, but right now they reside in perishing bodies—a situation that can only be awkward and frustrating.

And so we wait and we hope. We hope because we are works in progress, and although our salvation is complete, we have more good things coming. What a wonderful freedom and completion we will experience when we are redeemed in full, both body and soul. Maybe we will look back on our restless anticipation from the waiting room and realize that if we had only known what lay ahead, we would have worried less about our ailing earthly bodies and rejoiced more that a glorious body would one day be ours.

Keep your hope alive by looking forward to the day when aging, ill bodies are but a distant memory. And, if you're spending a lot of time in waiting rooms, be sure to bring a book.

Dear Father in Heaven,
I have glimpsed just enough of heaven through your
Holy Spirit to know that wondrous freedom and peace
lie ahead. Yet while my soul is free in you, my body
still concerns me, hinders me, and keeps me earthbound.
While I wait for heaven, give me hope and courage.
In Jesus' name. Amen.

Psalm for the Soul

I am feeble and utterly crushed;
I groan in anguish of heart.
All my longings lie open before you, O Lord;
my sighing is not hidden from you. (Ps. 38:8–9)

Solid Hope

*A faith and knowledge resting on the hope of eternal life, which
God, who does not lie, promised before the beginning of time.*
TITUS 1:2

*H*ope is an elusive concept that is used in a variety of
ways. A friend might say, "I hope you'll be well soon,"
or, "I hope this new treatment will be effective." We
even associate hope with such timeworn phrases as "hope springs
eternal," or "where there's life, there's hope." After a while the
meaning is so muddled that it sparks no solid reality. Yet hope is a
constant element spoken of in the Bible. Is there really a difference
in the believer's hope and wishing on a star?

Hope in and of itself has little significance. We can hope to win
the lottery, but the fulfillment of that desire is left totally to chance
and, therefore, not well-founded. In other words, what are we hoping in? What gives hope strength and meaning is its object. When
we submit our body to the care of a doctor, we are placing hope in
his training, skill, and knowledge. Most of the time that hope is
reasonable. Medical personnel do the best they can for us and often
are able to restore us to improved health. Other times, regardless
of their best efforts, our hopes are failed. We discover that despite
our hopes, resources are limited and doctors and nurses are fallible.

Christians have many hopes that make up their faith: there is
the hope for salvation, the rapture of the church, the appearing of
Jesus Christ, the hope for righteousness, the hope of heaven, and
more. All of these hopes rest upon the fundamental hope of eternal
life promised to us by God that begins when we put our faith in
Jesus Christ. At that moment of faith, we may only grasp that our
soul has been saved, but eventually we understand that we also
have the promise of the resurrection of the body to look forward
to. Our hopes are based in large part on our understanding and
trust in the character of God.

Paul tells us that there is an excellent reason for solid hope because God "does not lie." When he makes a promise, we can be sure that the promise will be fulfilled. At a time in life when many of the things we have placed our hope in have failed and fallen away, what an awesome assurance to be rooted in timeless, changeless truth. It is in the happy anticipation of eternal life with Christ that the ultimate hope of the believer rests.

Even if hope is fading in the restoration of your health, if you're a believer in Jesus Christ, you have a valid, vital hope for the future based on a trustworthy God. The same God who raised Jesus from the dead and glorified him is the One in whom you have placed your hope. You can trust in that; you can rest in that.

Heavenly Father,
I can become so distracted with the focus on my
physical health that I reach the point of losing
track of more important things. I hope that I can be
made well, but I know that eventually I, like every
human being, will die. You have promised me a glorious
life that changes at the moment of death and commences
in a new and glorious way. Thank you for that hope,
hope that is as sure as you. Amen.

Psalm for the Soul

Be strong and take heart,
all you who hope in the LORD. (Ps. 31:24)

Where to Turn

*"Come to me, all you who are weary and burdened,
and I will give you rest."*
MATTHEW 11:28

Mom fought cancer for fifteen years. *Fought* was indeed the operative word. We approached this enemy with an attitude of waging warfare. At the onset of each new battle, we came to the doctor with the steady resolve of soldiers prepared to hunker down and use the available medical weaponry until the enemy once again had been forced back into submission.

There are few human conditions so burdensome and exhausting as coping with life-threatening illness. When faced with such an adversary, we enter into a grueling regimen of tests, treatments, medicines, side effects, doctor appointments, and hospitalizations. But we are not alone in our battle; we go to war standing shoulder to shoulder with family, friends, the doctor, and the knowledge of the medical community.

There may come a time, however, when the arsenal of ammunition is exhausted, and the enemy is still advancing. A subtle change in the doctor's demeanor confirms our own suspicions. Eventually, she concedes that there is no longer hope of even a temporary victory. The time has come to lay down our weapons.

For the patient the full weight of the illness bears down with oppressive force. Even though family will still be by your side, even though doctors assure they will be there to help, there is a feeling of utter isolation.

When all the trusted avenues of support can no longer help, where do you turn?

"Come to me," Jesus says.

He doesn't urge us to go to church, call a Christian friend, or listen to a pastor on the radio. This is a unique moment when Jesus calls and we answer on his terms—alone and in total dependence and total submission. When others are sadly turning away, he beckons us with welcoming comfort and hope:

Come to me if you're exhausted by the drudgery of struggle. Come to me if illness is ending your life. Come to me if you can no longer lift, much less carry the burden. I will carry your sorrows and fears. I will carry you! Come to me. Come to me.

The Christian life is not a passive giving in to the inevitability of death. Rather, it is eagerly reaching past death to take hold of Jesus and his promise of eternal life. We are ready because we possess the deep soul-peace of confident assurance that our sins have been forgiven and paid for by the death and resurrection of our Savior. Yes, the battle for life on this plane is over, but we stand victorious at the threshold of a new life—one that will never end.

Father in Heaven,
I don't want to wait until my failing health drives me to you in desperation. I come to you now, seeking your forgiveness and the certainty of eternal life. Let me live with the confidence that because of the sacrifice of your sinless life, my death will mean that I can enter a new and finer life. Thank you for offering true hope, relief from the struggle, and rest for my soul. Amen.

Psalm for the Soul

My soul finds rest in God alone;
my salvation comes from him. (Ps. 62:1)

Parting Blessings

*By faith Jacob, when he was dying, blessed each of Joseph's sons,
and worshiped as he leaned on the top of his staff.*
HEBREWS 11:21

I collect antique Bibles. I like the small ones that would have
been carried to church or cradled in the hands as one read
by the fire. Sometimes the Bibles have inscriptions that provide a glimpse into both the giver and the recipient. The message in
one of my favorite old Bibles reads:

My dear little Neddie, not quite three years old. Your
dying mother leaves you this little precious Bible. You
must love and keep it for her sake.

Come to Jesus little one,
come to Jesus now.
He will take you in his arms,
And bind you on his brow.
—H. W. Burns, Feb. 1864

There is no telling the impact this mother's prayer and blessing
had on her son as he grew and matured. If he remembered nothing
else, the Bible and its message would always remind him of what
his mother found most important to impart to him before she died.

When Jacob was dying, Joseph and his two sons came to be by
his side. Joseph wanted to comfort his father, but he also wanted to
receive a blessing for himself and his two sons. Jacob willingly
complied: "May the God before whom my fathers Abraham and
Isaac walked, the God who has been my shepherd all my life to this
day, the Angel who has delivered me from all harm—may he bless
these boys. May they be called by my name and the names of my
fathers Abraham and Isaac, and may they increase greatly upon the
earth" (Gen. 48:15–16).

What a touching and remarkable blessing! Joseph's two sons
were young men on the brink of adulthood. This deathbed blessing

and witness of their grandfather's faith surely had a lifelong impact on them. Jacob had led a life of faith, and at the end of his life, when faith was greatly needed, it enabled him to finish well.

Fears may have prevented us from stating the testimony of our faith and the goodness of God in our life. It's not too late to challenge those fears. Think about it: Who wouldn't want a blessing from someone they love? Who wouldn't cherish the memory of encouragement and hope from one who has experienced the highs and lows of a lifetime?

What would you inscribe on the flyleaf of a Bible to someone you love deeply? A statement of your hope and faith may well resonate through the generations.

Heavenly Father,
Like Jacob, I am weary, yet I want to bless those
I love by leaving them a legacy of faith. As I gather
my strength and courage to speak of my love for you,
meet me with your courage and your strength so that
I am able. My weakness does not prevent me from
worshiping you deep within my spirit. Amen.

Psalm for the Soul
May God be gracious to us and bless us
and make his face shine upon us. (Ps. 67:1)

Procrastination's Price

Several days later Felix came with his wife Drusilla, who was
a Jewess. He sent for Paul and listened to him as he spoke
about faith in Christ Jesus. As Paul discoursed on righteousness,
self-control and the judgment to come, Felix was afraid and
said, "That's enough for now! You may leave. When I find
it convenient, I will send for you."

ACTS 24:24–25

When I was in college, I inevitably waited until the last minute to study or do my homework. As a result, I often had frenzied periods of near panic as I struggled to get things done. There is, however, a far more serious kind of procrastination that can have eternal consequences. The biblical account of Felix and Drusilla provides a perfect illustration.

The Apostle Paul had been put into prison on charges that he was a nuisance and troublemaker. The prosecuting attorney stated a list of bogus charges and laced his discourse with plenty of flattery, hoping to sway the "most excellent" governor, Felix. Paul was allowed to speak on his own behalf and effectively defended his innocence, but to placate the Jews, Felix delayed a decision and returned Paul to prison.

In truth, Felix was neither an excellent governor nor an excellent person. He was tyrannical and oppressive in his governing, and, in his personal life, his only goal was to satisfy his own desires. Drusilla had been married to the king of Emesa when Felix persuaded her to leave her husband and marry him. But despite their callused attitudes, Paul's speech had pricked the couple's curiosity about Christianity as was evidenced when Felix later sent for Paul and asked him to speak privately to them about faith in Jesus.

Paul's sermon was tailor-made for them. Even though as a prisoner, Paul was dependent on Felix, he boldly spoke about righteousness, self-control, and the judgment to come. In response, the governor was alarmed. It was clear that he was neither righteous, in control of his desires, nor ready for eternal judgment. God's Word was piercing his conscience and showing his need for repentance and salvation. But rather than respond to this precious urging, Felix said, "That's enough for now! You may leave. When I find it convenient, I will send for you." There is no indication that a more convenient time ever arrived.

Most of us have our own ways of dulling our ability to hear God and respond quickly to his urgings. Sometimes we put it off for something as trivial as watching TV or thinking about business, our friends, or our health. In truth, as we grow older and our habits are more deeply ingrained, it becomes harder and harder to be open to the Lord.

Does thinking about judgment and eternity make you tremble? If so, don't put it off another minute, turn away from your sins right now and humbly receive Jesus Christ as your Lord and your Savior.

Father God,
Now is the time finally to agree with you that I am
a sinner who needs a Savior. Forgive me and come into
my heart this moment. I don't want to procrastinate
another instant, and I certainly don't want to face eternity
without you. Thank you for the sacrifice of your Son,
Jesus Christ, so that I can be at peace and at home with
you forever. In Jesus' name. Amen.

Psalm for the Soul

Today, if you hear his voice,
do not harden your hearts. (Ps. 95:7–8)

The Look of Perseverance

Blessed is the man who perseveres under trial, because when he has stood the test, he will receive the crown of life that God has promised to those who love him.
JAMES 1:12

Years ago, Gloria Steinhem, a feminist leader and the editor of *Ms.* magazine, was giving a speech around the same time she had reached a milestone birthday. A reporter commented that she didn't look forty years old, to which she replied, "This is what forty looks like."

I've always liked that answer because it rejected stereotypical thinking and forced a reevaluation of our perceptions and beliefs. We may think we know what it means to be forty, fifty, or eighty years of age, but do we? Now stretch that thought, and try to imagine how someone would look who has *persevered* under trials. Difficult, isn't it?

Earlier in chapter one, James gives us some guidelines. He tells us that perseverance is developed when our faith is tested, and by enduring our trials, perseverance has the opportunity to "finish its work" (v. 4). We can assume, then, that perseverance is an active process rather than a passive gritting of teeth and waiting for the trial to be over. The Lord views perseverance as an important character trait that can transform the journey of our suffering into a pathway to blessings. Therefore, it's important that we know what perseverance in the life of a believer looks like.

Perseverance looks like maturity. Maturity enables us to look beyond our present suffering and focus on the end result. Yes, we are experiencing trouble, but God has lifted it out of the mundane by giving it the divine function of polishing the rough edges of our faith. Naturally, Satan has opposite goals and wants our suffering to pull us into the snare of self-pity and sin, but God's purpose is to fill the gaps of our faith and solidify our devotion to him (v. 4).

Perseverance looks like wisdom. The persevering individual will ask God for wisdom when he feels it lacking in his life. Perhaps he doesn't understand his current trials, but although he is perplexed, he trusts God and wants to cooperate and surrender to his purpose for allowing them (v. 5).

Perseverance looks like love. Rather than succumbing to self-pity, one who perseveres keeps his love for God and God's love for him firmly fixed in his mind. He reminds himself that Jesus loves him so much that he purchased him at the price of his own blood. Therefore, his Lord will never abandon him regardless of what trials may come his way (v. 12).

God honors our faithful perseverance by blessing us both now and in the future. In this life we are blessed by the stabilizing qualities that come through perseverance, and when we reach heaven, we are promised a crown of life. The world may not understand our quiet strength and steady faith of perseverance, but if we are asked, we can answer, "This is what following Jesus looks like."

Holy Father,
I want to stand the tests that come my way. I know
I can do that only by steady reliance on you and your
promises. Let me trample disruptive doubt with the
solid facts of who you are and your faithfulness. Amen.

Psalm for the Soul
My comfort in my suffering is this:
Your promise preserves my life. (Ps. 119:50)

The Perspective of Paul

For me, to live is Christ and to die is gain.
PHILIPPIANS 1:21

Perspective is everything. Paul didn't write this bold statement from an overstuffed chair in a cozy home surrounded by caring friends. Instead, Paul was isolated in a harsh Roman prison where he was being persecuted for his faith in Christ. Death was not a remote notion that would happen to him *someday*. Suffering was a daily fact of his life, and death was a very real possibility.

When death draws near, the true objects of our affection become clear. If we have devoted our life to the accumulation of wealth, we see the futility of our possessions in light of eternity. If we have lived for pleasures, we find that they are suddenly absent in our need. If we have lived for personal achievements and the prestige of fame, we see that they are fickle and our accomplishments are quickly and easily forgotten. But when we live for Christ, as Paul did, death becomes the culminating event that brings us into his presence. Death, that robber of earthly pleasures, becomes the vehicle of our personal gain.

It might be tempting to assume that Paul's light touch on the world was the result of having few emotional attachments, but that was not so: "How I long for all of you with the affection of Christ Jesus" (v. 8). As was evidenced in his obvious love for the believers in Philippi, Paul had meaningful relationships with people he loved, but they did not blind him to the bigger picture. He knew that eventually all of his loved ones would die, and then they would be together again—as they most certainly are to this day.

In this life our relationship to the Lord depends greatly on our commitment to seek him daily and commune with him through studying the Bible and praying. But when we have left the confines of mortal life, we enter into an easy fellowship where we are unhindered by a human body, sin, and the concerns of the world. We are simply and gloriously *with* him.

Paul's choice: "To live is Christ, and to die is gain" was really but one choice—Jesus Christ. Either way he was devoted to his Lord; either way he was victorious.

> *Lord God,*
> *I want to develop the perspective of Paul. You have*
> *put eternity in my heart; enable me also to put it in my*
> *mind so that I can travel through this time of my life with*
> *dignity, hope, and joy. Since I cannot choose the time*
> *of my death, my only choice is to live fully for you. Amen.*

Psalm for the Soul

I will not die but live,
and will proclaim what the LORD has done. (Ps. 118:17)

The Way to Heaven

Jesus answered, "I am the way and the truth and the life.
No one comes to the Father except through me."
JOHN 14:6

I'm always fascinated to hear accounts of individuals who
have attempted to climb Mount Everest. In spite of ava-
lanches, ice crevasses, wind, and blinding snow, they press
on and follow their guide on the determined path in hopes that they
will safely reach the summit.

Before pursuing such a monumental goal, one thing is certain:
the climbers prepare intensely and leave as little as possible to
chance. These adventurers purchase the best clothing, the finest
equipment, and scrupulously plan their food and water needs. For
at least a year before the climb, they prepare physically in a disciplined regimen of aerobics and weight training.

But all these preparations would be totally useless if the most
vital element of their journey were neglected: finding an experienced guide who knows the way. Can you imagine setting out for
the summit and saying, "Oh, I'll just start climbing upward. It
doesn't really matter which way I go"? Chances are that by the end
of the first day, that individual would be hopelessly lost and perhaps forfeit his life for his careless arrogance.

Any thoughtful person would know that such foolish confidence and disregard of the risks would result in disaster rather
than a successful climb. Isn't it interesting, then, that we tolerate
and encourage these same cavalier attitudes when on a quest to
find God?

Jesus made clear that he is the only Guide who can show us the
way to God the Father and eternal life in heaven. He never even
remotely suggests that all roads lead to heaven or that any sincere
belief will be accepted and honored by God.

When we examine God's plan, we understand why. From the very beginning, God knew that sinful mankind could never reach his perfect standard of holiness in other words, on our own merit, we could never be good enough for heaven. But God loved us so much that he found a way for us to be with him. He gave his perfect Son, Jesus, to bear our sins as if he had committed them himself. He then took our punishment and died on the cross so that we could escape eternal punishment and reach heaven on the basis of Christ's work and our relationship to him.

The path to the heavenly summit has been marked with the precious blood of Jesus Christ. At such a priceless cost, trying to get there any other way would insult God and trample Christ's sacrificial work.

Nothing is hidden about finding the way to heaven. Jesus said that *he* is the way to heaven. He doesn't simply point the way; he *is* the way. And "no one" (not even one!), said Jesus, "comes to the Father except through me."

> *Father God,*
> *I see that trying to find my way to heaven apart*
> *from your Son, Jesus, is foolish arrogance. I have*
> *been walking on the slippery edge of a cliff. Forgive*
> *me for my pride that has kept me from receiving you*
> *earlier in my life. I pray that you will now come into*
> *my heart and be my Lord and my Guide in this life and*
> *the life to come. In Jesus' name. Amen.*

Psalm for the Soul

Into your hands I commit my spirit;
redeem me, O LORD, the God of truth. (Ps. 31:5)

Awaiting the Faithful: A Crown

"Be faithful, even to the point of death,
and I will give you the crown of life."
REVELATION 2:10

On April 20, 1999, Rachel Scott drove to her high school in Denver as she had on so many other days. But on this day, seventeen-year-old Rachel would be confronted with the choice of being faithful to her beliefs even to the point of death. Two male students had staged an attack and were murdering students and teachers. With a gun pointed at her head, Rachel was taunted and questioned about her belief in God. When she confirmed those beliefs, she was shot and killed.

Most of us will never face such a dramatic testing of our beliefs even though each one of us will one day confront the testing that comes with death. At that time, what can we do to prove ourselves faithful to our God? Sometimes the most we can do under extreme pressure is to hold fast to our faith and firmly confess Jesus Christ as our Savior. As others watch us, what they outwardly see may be our devotion to the Word of God and our dedication to trusting him in the face of death.

Although these actions may not seem particularly heroic, the Lord himself promises to give us the crown of life in return for our faithfulness. This idea is expanded upon in the New Testament book of James: "Blessed is the man who perseveres under trial, because when he has stood the test, he will receive the crown of life that God has promised to those who love him" (James 1:12). The trial may be a direct assault on our spiritual convictions, or it may be the subtle but taxing pressure that comes from increasing weakness and decreasing health. Our determination to rise to those circumstances with faith can turn the mundane into the inspirational.

There is no doubt that in this earthly realm we will all have trials and troubles. But our ability to balance the troubles of today in the context of the certainty of eternity with Christ can keep us from succumbing to despair and hopelessness. When we love the Lord more than we fear pain and rejection now, heaven will hold for us a special reward.

Does it seem strange to think about being individually acknowledged in heaven? After all, won't heaven be the same for everyone who is there? The Bible indicates that within that atmosphere of joy, peace, and worship, God will continue to deal with us as individuals and in accordance to our love and faithful actions.

Jesus reminded us that our trials and persecutions on earth are comparatively short when viewed through the lens of our awaiting eternal joy. Never was that more true than for Rachel Scott. There is no doubt that although she died young, she has been given the crown of life, and even now she is living out the promise of her own middle name: Joy.

Heavenly Father,
Give me the courage to hold on tight to the beliefs
that have sustained me through my life. You have
promised to strengthen those who are weak, so I ask
you to bolster my faith so that when I am in your presence,
you will greet me with your crowning love.
In Jesus' name. Amen.

Psalm for the Soul

For the LORD loves the just
and will not forsake his faithful ones. (Ps. 37:28)

Faithful Thanks

*Be joyful always; pray continually; give thanks in all circum-
stances, for this is God's will for you in Christ Jesus.*
1 THESSALONIANS 5:16

I love the story in Luke 17 that tells of Jesus healing the ten
lepers. As Jesus was traveling along the border between
Samaria and Galilee, ten leprous men called to him from a
distance and said, "Jesus, Master, have pity on us!" Perhaps
because of their faith in asking, Jesus didn't hesitate and directed
them to go show themselves to the priests. The priests had no function in the healing but only the power to pronounce that they were
cleansed of this highly contagious disease so they could rejoin
society. Therefore, still-leprous men took those first steps in the
direction of the priest. The actual healing took place as they walked
in faith.

One can't help imagining their excitement. They were probably running by the time they neared the temple. But one of the men,
after seeing that he was healed, turned away from the group and
came back to Jesus, praising him in a loud voice. "He threw himself at Jesus' feet and thanked him" (Luke 17:16).

The Lord noted that out of the ten, he was the only one who
returned to give God the glory and praise for healing him. "Then
he [Jesus] said to him, 'Rise and go; your faith has made you well'"
(v. 19). The man's praise was a spontaneous expression of his deep
appreciation and praise for God. How beautiful!

Only one tenth of the group of lepers gave thanks. If thankfulness is this rare in those who have received a miraculous healing, it
must be even more rare to praise and thank God for those conditions and circumstances that cause worry, sadness, and anxiety. But
this is exactly what we are instructed to do. Ephesians 5:20 tells us,
"Always giving thanks to God the Father for everything, in the
name of our Lord Jesus Christ." For everything? Yes, *everything!*

How long has it been since you thanked God for your present circumstances? If this seems absurd to you, remember that obedience and gratitude are directly linked. As you obediently thank God for your situation, you will begin to discern the hidden blessings that are a direct result of your suffering. For instance, through experiencing tribulation, we are often able to understand and see God's purpose more clearly. Then, as we pray, we are lifted out of our circumstances to freshly experience the joy of God in the face of Christ Jesus. Like a divine chain reaction, through obedient and faithful thanks, our thankfulness abounds, and we are able to give boundless thanks to God.

Heavenly Father,
When I can't see any reason to give you thanks, help
me remember that it is a command with a divine purpose.
I want to start praising you and thanking you right now
from the depths of my hard circumstances, rather than
waiting until my circumstances have changed to my
satisfaction before I give you the praise and honor
that you are due. Your Word tells me that rejoicing,
constant prayer, and giving thanks are the will of
God in Christ Jesus. I don't just want a healed body;
I want a soul fit for the glories of heaven.
Thank you, Lord Jesus! Amen.

Psalm for the Soul
I will give thanks to the LORD because of his righteousness and will sing praise to the name of the LORD Most High. (Ps. 7:17)

Resurrection Hope

Praise be to the God and Father of our Lord Jesus Christ!
In his great mercy he has given us new birth into a living hope
through the resurrection of Jesus Christ from the dead.

1 PETER 1:3

Nothing invests us in the future like our children and grand-children. When my children were born, I not only experienced a new kind of love; I felt a new interest and hope in the future. I was no longer above the fray of the world's problems because now my own children would have to function, flourish, and survive in it.

Hope in the resurrection follows a similar pattern. When we, or someone we love, face death, our beliefs about resurrection with Jesus suddenly become more than passive facts of our faith.

But before we can possess a hope for resurrection after death, we must be sure there has been the second birth—a spiritual birth in Jesus. If that has not happened, there is simply no hope for resurrection. When we are born again by receiving Jesus Christ as Savior, we become God's very own. At that moment of surrender, we are resurrected into a new realm of life. We are newly aware of God, and we hunger for him and his purpose for our life. As we grow more into the likeness of Jesus, our lives are transformed. Then, when we enter eternity, we come into the promise of resurrection.

Although death is still frightening, Jesus mapped out this territory for us in advance and took remarkable steps to demystify it. In the most public and humiliating of circumstances, Jesus died. His body was removed from the cross and prepared for burial. For three dark days the tomb was sealed. Then, on the third day, Jesus walked out of the tomb and into our lives again as our resurrected Lord who had accomplished the mighty work of our redemption.

Believers sometimes wear the cross to remind themselves of Jesus' death that should have been their own, but it is the empty tomb that propels us in hope toward the next and lasting phase of life. Paul tells us that, "The body that is sown is perishable, it is raised imperishable; it is sown in dishonor, it is raised in glory; it is sown in weakness, it is raised in power; it is sown a natural body, it is raised a spiritual body" (1 Cor. 15:42–44). This is solid testimony to God's plan and promise. This is resurrection hope.

Holy Father,
Your resurrection and transformation were magnificent
and brimming with hope and promise. I, too, am destined
for resurrection because I have received you as my Savior
and have been born again. Right now, help me keep
this hope alive in my heart until such time as I receive
the promise in its fullness. In Jesus' name. Amen.

Psalm for the Soul

I wait for the LORD, my soul waits,
and in his word I put my hope. (Ps. 130:5)

Good Deeds

You are not your own; you were bought at a price.
I CORINTHIANS 6:19–20

O f all the fundamental rights that Americans cherish, personal freedom is perhaps the dearest. We prize our liberty and stand ready to defend it or fight for it when we are under the threat of oppression and slavery.

As a nation, however, we are not innocent of the crime we most fear. We share the shame of having participated in slavery and failing to honor the freedom and dignity of others. As the memory of slavery recedes into the shadows of time, the reality of the horror of it fades as well. But recently it was brought vividly to my mind when I saw copies of archived deeds that dispassionately listed human beings as mere property.

In 1844, one such deed was filed in book 54, page 167 of Mason County, Kentucky. In it, three little girls and one little boy are listed by first name only and described simply by their race, sex, and approximate ages. The narrative that follows the listing reads: "This conveyance to be in trust for the proper use and benefit of Edward Robertson's daughter, Agnes Keith, wife of Charles Keith, for her life with remainder in fee to the children of her body. She is to have the entire use and control of the said slaves during her life. In case of her death before her children arrive at full age, paid trustee is to control said slaves."

Simply stated, these four children were destined to be slaves of the current and future generations of their owners. There was no end to their servitude.

The Christian life, in both amazing similarity and contrast, demonstrates the paradox of the freedom that comes from being slaves of Christ. The Apostle Paul counseled believers on this subject: "Were you a slave when you were called? Don't let it trouble you—although if you can gain your freedom, do so. For he who was a slave when he was called by the Lord is the Lord's freedman; similarly, he who was a free man when he was called is Christ's slave" (1 Cor. 7:21–22). A clear reminder that if we are slaves to man, we are still free in Christ, and if we are free men, we are yet servants of Christ.

We were bought at the price of his priceless blood and deeded to him for eternity. Regardless of our station in this life, we are not our own. Our precious slavery means that we are occupied by the Spirit of God. This gives us a deep perspective whether we are living in a vital, healthy body or standing at the threshold of eternity. We are not our own, but we are entirely free.

Lord God,
I feel captive by my poor health and diminishing abilities.
Thank you for buying me with your precious blood so that
I can be your very own, for now and forever.
In Jesus name. Amen.

Psalm for the Soul

As the eyes of slaves look to the hand of their master,
as the eyes of a maid look to the hand of her mistress,
so our eyes look to the LORD our God,
till he shows us his mercy. (Ps. 123:2)

Reversal of Fortune

*The brother in humble circumstances ought to take pride in his
high position. But the one who is rich should take pride in
his low position, because he will pass away like a wild flower.*
JAMES 1:9–10

Circumstances of great poverty or great wealth can sometimes bring serious problems. God knew that extreme situations presented a particular temptation to the believer, so
through the inspiration of the Holy Spirit, James has told us how
to maintain a balanced perspective even in the midst of highs and
lows.

Every condition of life has its challenges, but James points out
that no circumstance, regardless of how dire, can prevent us from
worshipping God. The poor believer can rejoice that she has true,
incorruptible wealth. She is an heir of God and a joint heir with
Jesus Christ. Despite her humble surroundings, she is destined for
a glorious eternal kingdom. Because poverty causes her to be
dependent for the necessities of life, walking by faith and trust may
already be a well-ingrained part of life.

Conversely, the rich believer may be tempted to decide she
doesn't need God because of the comfort and insulation from many
problems that her wealth provides. But James tells the rich not to
take pride in their wealth but instead to rejoice in the humbling
knowledge that life is fragile and fleeting and there is a greater purpose than amassing riches.

These same truths are valid when health has failed and we are
immersed in illness. If we have always been well, suddenly being ill
can feel shattering. It is a comfort to remember that part of our
heavenly inheritance will include an incorruptible body and the
absence of suffering and pain. Until then we can be sure that God
is near in our suffering.

Struggles with money or health, as tough as they are, may be for the divine purposes of revealing the true state of our soul and driving us to attend to the matter of getting right with God. As sinners, we were destined for death and separation from God, but Jesus, in the ultimate reversal of fortune, offers us the incredible gift of life with him for eternity. He has done the redeeming work on the cross and extended his hand, but we must reach out to take it.

Holy Father,
I hunger for truth, and you are faithful to provide it
in your Word. Help me remember that in the grand
scheme of things, my life is as fragile and short-lived as
a wildflower. I know that you are at the heart of anything
that prompts me to settle the question of where I will spend
eternity. Regardless of the state of my finances or my
health, I know that my unchanging riches and eternal
life are in Christ. In Jesus' name. Amen.

Psalm for the Soul

Each man's life is but a breath.
Man is a mere phantom as he goes to and fro:
He bustles about, but only in vain;
he heaps up wealth, not knowing who will get it. (Ps. 39:5–6)

Look Up!

I lift up my eyes to the hills—
where does my help come from?
My help comes from the LORD,
the Maker of heaven and earth.
PSALM 121:1–2

O utside my dining room window I can see the peak of the mountain that borders the city on the east. I love to look toward that majestic sight and realize that my Lord drew it up from the depths of the earth at creation. Sometimes the mountain is blanketed in clouds that reach over the crest like gloved fingers; other times the setting sun turns it a brilliant watermelon pink that seems to glow from the depths of its core. But despite its changing appearance, it is a reminder of God's steadfast command over all the elements and events of this world and the ever-changing circumstances of my life.

The psalmist held a similar vision, and when his eyes were lifted up to those hills, it had the effect of diminishing his cares and troubles, if only for a few moments. He was reminded that the mountains he gazed upon were made by the Lord who also made the awaiting, unseen, glories of heaven. Therefore, all his current concerns and future hopes were held firmly in God's grasp.

What comfort for the believer to know that no accident or adversity will occur that is outside God's control or jurisdiction. Even if the night is disturbed by unforeseen trouble, it is not a surprise to our God, who never slumbers. His watchfulness provides shade from the heat of oppressive illness; in the icy loneliness of sorrow and loss, his Word dwells in us and warms us from the heart out.

What lasting harm can come to us? Illness? Death? The Lord watched over us as we came into the world, and certainly he will watch over us as we leave this world. We know the facts of our birth and life up to this time, but our heavenly Father knows our future and our earthly end in minute detail. Regardless of how we die, the Lord has disarmed the power of death by giving us eternal life.

To the naked eye, Christians go through the peaks and valleys of life and eventual death just like everyone else. However, what cannot be so easily observed is the way God uses these occurrences in our life to work toward an unseen good for other believers and for ourselves.

If you are weighed down with sadness, illness, and the fear of oncoming death, look up! Lift your eyes up to the hills where the Maker of heaven and earth has everything, every earthly detail, including you, his precious child, firmly in his hand.

Father God,
Sometimes when I try to lift up my eyes to see you,
it seems as though you are shrouded in mist. Clear away
the fog so that I can have a vision of you that is unhindered
by my circumstances. Like Moses, who wrote this psalm,
I pray that you will keep me from all harm and that
you will watch over my life until such time as I am safely
in your presence forevermore. In Jesus' name. Amen.

Psalm for the Soul

May you be blessed by the LORD,
the Maker of heaven and earth. (Ps. 115:15)

A Place Prepared

*"Do not let your hearts be troubled. Trust in God; trust
also in me. In my Father's house are many rooms; if it
were not so, I would have told you. I am going there
to prepare a place for you."*
JOHN 14:1-2

During Mom's stay in a skilled nursing facility following
surgery, she awoke one morning with a heavy feeling in
her chest. I was at home getting ready when a nurse
called and told me Mom was being taken by ambulance to the hospital. But after being there a few days and undergoing several tests,
no heart problem was found.

We breathed a sigh of relief. At least this was one problem we
didn't have to deal with. However, when I spoke with the administrator of the nursing facility to tell her we would be returning,
I learned that during Mom's absence her room had been given to
someone else. She didn't foresee having a place for her in the near
future.

I was stunned and Mom was upset. She still needed nursing
care, so I immediately set out to find a new place for her. I hated to
think that Mom would have to leave the roommate she got along
with so well and the now familiar staff. There had been so many
changes in her life recently, and now it looked as though there
would be more. I prayed that God would guide my steps and
quickly help me find a place for her.

Jesus cares about such things. He knows it is essential to our
well-being to know that our living needs are met. When Jesus comforted his disciples, they had just been told that he was leaving
them alone. They felt abandoned and confused, so Jesus assured
them not to worry. They were accustomed to trusting the unseen
God; therefore, it should be easier to trust in him whom they had
seen.

Then Jesus made a deeply comforting promise. He said that there is a place prepared for each of us in his Father's house. Our arrival is a much-anticipated and joyful event. Jesus himself will prepare for it. Unlike the inn in Bethlehem that turned away Mary as she was about to deliver, right now there is a room ready and waiting just for us.

Despite our upset over Mom's situation, before the day was over, the Lord answered my prayer. The administrator called to say she had made some creative changes, and Mom could return to her own room. All in all, this stressful experience reminded me that when we are at home in heaven no clerical error or red tape will send us scurrying for interim lodging until our needs synchronize with someone else. We will never feel that our presence has caused a hardship or put someone out. At long last we will be home, surrounded by perfect comfort, peace, beauty—and our loving Lord Jesus.

Holy Father,
Sometimes I feel like such a burden. I know that people
are doing their jobs, but I long to feel at home—to feel
welcomed, cherished, anticipated, and loved. Give those
who are helping me both wisdom and compassion. And
give me peace and joy in the knowledge that even now
you have a place prepared for me in heaven.
In Jesus' name. Amen.

Psalm for the Soul
Blessed are those who dwell in your house;
they are every praising you. (Ps. 84:4)

Severe Blessings

"Shall we accept good from God, and not trouble?"
JOB 2:10

*I*t reads like the script of a soap opera. In rapid succession Job's oxen and donkeys were attacked and taken, and his servants were killed. No sooner had he heard this than fire took his sheep and the servants tending them. Next his camels were gone and more servants were killed. Then, finally, all his sons and daughters were killed.

Job was distraught. With knees weak from grief, he fell to the ground and cried, "Naked I came from my mother's womb, and naked I will depart. The LORD gave and the LORD has taken away; may the name of the LORD be praised" (1:21).

The Bible allows us to pull back the curtain of heaven and see what was really going on with this extreme situation. Satan had challenged God regarding the true character of Job. He made the charge that Job was righteous and revered God only because God protected and blessed him.

Through the course of Satan's testings, Job proved him wrong. In spite of his severe losses, he continued to praise and trust God. Job was unaware that he had a heavenly audience, and the Lord was monitoring every movement and setting Satan's limits along the way. It was obvious to God and Satan that Job had responded as a righteous man under these circumstances, so Satan upped the ante. With the Lord's permission he attacked Job's body with excruciating boils from head to toe. Satan reasoned, "A man will give all he has for his own life . . . strike his flesh . . . and he will surely curse you to your face" (2:4–5).

At this low point temptation came through a particularly influential source: Job's wife. Certainly, she too, was grieving and distraught when she urged him to "curse God and die" (2:9). But Job responded, saying, "Shall we accept good from God, and not trouble?"

Good question. Personally I don't recall ever praying that God would send me trouble that would ultimately grow my patience, refine my character, deepen my commitment to him, create compassion for fellow sufferers, or propel me into mature faith. But during times of trouble, our faithful Father does just that. He continues to bless us with severe blessings that uniquely captivate our energy and attention and chisel our sloppy characters into a greater likeness of his Son, Jesus.

Shall we accept good from God and not trouble? For believers, even our trouble is transformed into blessings by our gracious Father who works them together for our good.

Heavenly Father,
Even on my worst day, I have basked in your blessings
of fresh air, sunlight, friends, freedom, and nature. With
both hands I have grabbed good things from your
generous Spirit. Now that I am in the midst of pain, I pray
that I will humbly accept this trouble and remain
faithfully devoted to you. In Jesus' name. Amen.

Psalm for the Soul

But you, O God, do see trouble and grief;
you consider it to take it in hand. (Ps. 10:14)

The Conqueror

No, in all these things we are more than conquerors
through him who loved us.
ROMANS 8:37

I met my friend Michael in the hospital on the cancer ward. We were admitted on the same day, and for several days following, we fought our separate battles to return to some measure of strength. One day, as I strolled the corridors pushing my IV stand, I noticed a Christian poster on the door at the end of the hall. I stood in the doorway and introduced myself to Michael and his large, friendly family. Michael was thirty-seven years old and a youth pastor from a small New Mexico town. He was dealing with a bone marrow disorder that would eventually require going out of state for a bone marrow transplant.

Understandably, we compared our illnesses and treatments, but soon our conversation turned from our physical conditions to our mutual love of the Lord. Over the next weeks we not only shared our prayer requests; we also shared Scriptures and insights the Lord was showing us. Once we even discovered that the Lord had led each of us to the same psalm and the same verse! It seemed as though God had made us friends and partners for the hard journeys we faced.

Our friendship blessed me with the freedom to be honest about my fears. One morning I was feeling particularly weak and discouraged. "Michael," I said, "do you ever consider that God may not choose to heal us?"

He thought for a minute. "Well, yes, but I try to turn those fears into faith. You know, the Bible says we are more than conquerors!"

In truth, that particular morning I felt like anything but a conqueror. I loved Michael's faith, and I fully believed that the Lord would cure his illness. I pictured years and years of powerful ministry ahead of him to proclaim God's goodness.

Eventually Michael went to California to start the transplant procedure. When days and then weeks passed without hearing from him, I suspected he was having trouble. Still, I was stunned when a call came to tell me that Michael had died while in the process of receiving his transplant.

I struggled to understand why this awesome young man of God was conquered by disease. In my sadness I turned to the passage in Romans that Michael had referred to: "No, in all these things we are more than conquerors through him who loved us." But it was the next verse that brought the comfort and peace I needed: "For I am convinced that neither death nor life, neither angels nor demons, neither the present nor the future, nor any powers, neither height nor depth, nor anything else in all creation, will be able to separate us from the love of God that is in Christ Jesus our Lord" (v. 38).

Michael was not *conquered* by disease or by death. All death had accomplished was to usher him into eternal life and bring him face-to-face with the Lord he loved. Through the work of Jesus on the cross, Michael was victorious over Satan's best efforts to separate him from the love of Jesus. I miss my friend, but I rejoice in his victory. He was, indeed, more than a conqueror.

Father God,
I am so earthbound in my perceptions of life and death.
Thank you for the promise that nothing, not even death,
can separate your children from your love.
In Jesus' name. Amen.

Psalm for the Soul

For great is his love toward us,
and the faithfulness of the LORD endures forever.
Praise the LORD. (Ps. 117:2)

The Spiritual Poor-Mouth

Praise be to the God and Father of our Lord Jesus Christ,
who has blessed us in the heavenly realms with
every spiritual blessing in Christ.
EPHESIANS 1:3

It's fascinating to hear stories of eccentric wealthy people who lived in virtual poverty. Such was a man named John G. Wendel, a New Yorker who was so determined to keep the family fortune within the family that neither he nor five of his six sisters ever married. When one of the sisters died in 1931, her estate was worth more than one hundred million dollars, yet she was living without electricity and had only one dress that she had made herself and worn for twenty-five years.

We scratch our heads and wonder why on earth anyone would choose poverty when riches were at her fingertips. But before we get too carried away pondering her foolishness, it might be wise to check ourselves and see if we have done the same thing.

Most of us are well aware of our finances and do our best to live within our means. But are we living in needless spiritual poverty, complaining that God doesn't care about us or isn't answering our prayers, while we sit on a fortune of unused, unacknowledged, and unappreciated blessings?

Paul reminds us that before we became children of God, we were dead in our sins, but in Christ we have been raised up and are securely settled in the heavenly places. God looks at us in this present life and sees us this way—not just as we are but the way we will be through eternity. Right now we may be walking through the places of this earthbound life, but in reality the eternal matter is settled.

Talk about riches! We've been chosen, forgiven, adopted, accepted, redeemed, sealed for eternity, granted an inheritance, and allowed to possess all the rights and privileges of a citizen of heaven. We have been, and continue to be, loved by the Creator of the universe!

In view of these facts, it's absurd to believe that God doesn't care about us and doesn't hear our prayers or choose to answer them. In the same way a father would be hurt and insulted by a son who had been given everything yet complained that his father had neglected him, it must hurt God when we ignore our spiritual riches. He gave his precious Son for us so that he could lavish the blessings of heaven on us. Why would he leave us lacking in lesser matters?

Heavenly Father,
I know I don't fully understand the riches that you've
given me through Jesus. I want to learn so that my life
will honor and please you. Fill me with your Holy Spirit
to help me grasp the truths in the Bible. Help me live
out my blessings that you've given so lovingly in your
Son, Jesus Christ. Amen.

Psalm for the Soul
Wealth and riches are in his house,
and his righteousness endures forever. (Ps. 112:3)

Vapor Trails

"You shall not bow down to them or worship them; for I, the
LORD *your God, am a jealous God, punishing the children for*
the sin of the fathers to the third and fourth generation of those
who hate me, but showing love to a thousand generations, of
those who love me and keep my commandments."
DEUTERONOMY 5:9–10

I am convinced that we have only a shallow understanding of
both the brevity and importance of life. We are creatures
of habit, lulled by the predictable days, hours, and minutes
that mark time. One day rarely distinguishes itself in memory from
the next.

When we are young, our lives seem to stretch endlessly before
us; but when we mature, we realize the fleeting nature of our frail
humanity. The Bible confirms this paradox of time by referring to
our lives as flowers that bloom and then fade or as mists or vapors.
"Why, you do not even know what will happen tomorrow. What
is your life? You are a mist that appears for a little while and then
vanishes" (James 4:14). But unlike the transient flower that blooms
and is forgotten, we have deep value to God and a lasting impact
on those we love.

Jonathan Edwards, the eighteenth-century revivalist, is a
remarkable illustration of the impact of one life devoted to Christ.
He was an instrumental force during the Great Awakening of
1740–1741 as well as being a writer and, eventually, the president
of Princeton University. Edwards and his wife, Sarah, were parents
of eleven children and were said to have had an ideal marriage.
Not only did Edwards influence untold thousands of people in his
lifetime, but he also had a profound effect on the future generations in his own family.

Benjamin B. Warfield, a Princeton scholar, has charted
Edwards' 1,394 known descendents. Among them there were

thirteen college presidents, sixty-five college professors, thirty judges, one hundred lawyers, sixty physicians, seventy-five army and navy officers, one hundred pastors, sixty authors, three United States senators, eighty public servants including governors and ministers to foreign countries, and one vice president of the United States.

It's hard to estimate the impact and value of one man who is devoted to Jesus Christ. Conversely, a life of selfish ambition, the pursuit of pleasure, disregard for loved ones, and ambivalence or hostility toward Christ can be equally destructive and deadening for generations as well.

There's no denying that our existence matters. We will leave a legacy of either blessings or pain. Our life may seem fleeting as we consider the fullness of time, but like a jet airplane that marks its path across the sky with a trail of vapor, we will leave a lasting mark on those we love.

Holy Father,
In the history of the world, no life or death has rivaled
the importance of Jesus. I am so thankful for the trail
of light he left for me to follow. I am often blinded by
the mundane quality of life, and I have missed countless
opportunities to show my devotion to you. Even now,
Lord, I pray that my remaining time on earth will be a
witness of my love and belief in you and will be a godly
legacy that reaches down through the generations. Amen.

Psalm for the Soul

You have made my days a mere handbreadth;
the span of my years is as nothing before you.
Each man's life is but a breath. (Ps. 39:5)

When Is It Too Late?

*Then he said, "Jesus, remember me when you come into
your kingdom." Jesus answered him, "I tell you the truth,
today you will be with me in paradise."*
LUKE 23:42–43

W. C. Fields made his mark on the American culture
during the Depression years. In his films he played a
hard-drinking, kid-and-animal-hating character who
was always quick with a muttered sarcasm. His real-life persona
didn't depart greatly from his screen image. When Fields died on
Christmas Day, 1946, several stories circulated about his last
words. The most popular of the rumors was that a visitor found
him in bed reading the Bible. When asked why he had a sudden
interest in the Bible, Fields replied, "I'm looking for loopholes."

If the story is true, we would be right to question the sincerity
of a man who didn't care to live his life for Christ but, when facing death, decided it might be a good idea to cover all the bases.

Only God knows a man's heart, and while there is good reason
to suspect Field's motives, the Bible gives us an account of a genuine deathbed conversion. As Jesus was being crucified, he hung
between two convicted thieves. One of the robbers, hardened and
angry, took the opportunity to hurl insults his way: "Aren't you the
Christ? Save yourself and us!" (Luke 23:39).

The other thief was deeply touched by Jesus and received him
in faith and reverence. He even rebuked the insolent thief: "'Don't
you fear God,' he said, 'since you are under the same sentence? We
are punished justly, for we are getting what our deeds deserve. But
this man has done nothing wrong'" (vv. 40–41).

Maybe this man had heard Jesus speak at an earlier time, or
maybe the sheer nearness to him made his own sin undeniable in
contrast to the Lord's righteousness. With the humility of a sinner
in the presence of a just God, he didn't presume to ask for a place

in heaven, but instead asked that Jesus simply "remember" him in his kingdom. He knew that to have a heavenly kingdom, Jesus must be King, and, therefore, he would also have the power over the thief's soul.

This was not someone looking for last-minute "loopholes." He was a sinner confessing his sin to a holy God. And God, who sees the heart, received him without reservation, without baptism, without communion, and without a life of good works. He received him just as he was.

Lord,
I sometimes wonder if it's too late for me. Like the man
on the cross, I see that I'm a thief, too. I've stolen my life,
which should have been lived for you, and used it for
my own purposes. Although I've rejected you in life,
I don't want to be separated from you for eternity.
I come to your cross now. Forgive me for the selfishness
that has blinded me to recognizing you, God, the Messiah.
Whether I die today or years from today, remember me,
and let me be with you in paradise. Amen.

Psalm for the Soul
Your kingdom is an everlasting kingdom,
and your dominion endures through all generations. (Ps. 145:13)

Angels in Waiting

*"The time came when the beggar died and
the angels carried him to Abraham's side."*
LUKE 16:22

There is a deathwatch in progress in the hospital room next door to mine. Late last night I heard the family members arriving, and I heard their weeping. Today, as I shuffled past their open door pushing my IV stand, I saw the form of a woman lying on the bed surrounded by a group of relatives and friends. My heart went out to them, but even as it did, I wondered if that same room might be flooded with a crowd of angelic beings sent on a special mission to carry the believer from this life into the presence of the Lord.

Scripture tells us that escorting believers to heaven is one of the functions of angels. In Luke's account of the rich man and Lazarus, we see angels actually fulfilling this work. The wealthy man is described as one who had trusted and worshipped his riches. He stands in sharp contrast with Lazarus who suffered humiliation, pain, and hunger. Safe within the luxury and security of his wealth, the rich man felt insulated from his need for God. Lazarus, the beggar, however, had apparently relied on God and placed his trust in him.

Eventually both men died. Although the rich man may have had a fine burial, he was ultimately cast into hell. The memory of riches and comfort now served as a painful counterpoint to his ever-present agony and thirst. For Lazarus, however, the difference must have been even more stunning. No longer did he grovel in the dirt at the gates of the wealthy man's home. No longer did painful sores torment him and alienate him from society. No longer did hunger drive him to eat the crumbs from another's table.

Even as Lazarus lay dying, angels hovered nearby ready to carry him to heaven. One can't help imagining the scene. Did they cool his brow with their sweet breath? Did the majestic winged beings surround him as the last gasps rattled in his chest? When Lazarus closed his eyes for the final time, did he open them to the glorious light of his heavenly transport as they cradled him in strong arms? Lazarus, a man who once begged bread and was attended by dogs, was now drinking of living water and reclining in fellowship with Father Abraham.

Meanwhile, the vigil next door continues. Are angels standing near? How very deceptive life can be! We look at the tangible and call it reality, but God's reality exceeds our limited vision and reaches deep into the glory of heaven.

Heavenly Father,
What an exciting and beautiful angelic ministry this is
to believers who are passing into eternal life. How loving
you are to provide for your children as they leave this
harsh world and enter your kingdom. Thank you for
these ministering spirits and their special mission.
In Jesus' name. Amen.

Psalm for the Soul
Praise him, all his angels,
praise him, all his heavenly hosts. (Ps. 148:2)

Defining Moments

"But what about you?" he asked.
"Who do you say I am?"
MATTHEW 16:15

I'm fascinated by the moments that come into our lives and bring with them the potential of changing our lives. Defining moments such as these can sometimes happen on a large scale and affect millions of people. There can be positive events like the invention of the printing press and the discovery of penicillin, or tragedies like the attacks on the World Trade Center and the Pentagon. Of the greatest fascination, however, is the often quiet but profound moment that takes place deep within the heart of an individual in response to God

In this passage of Scripture, we see Peter in his moment. He and the other disciples had been with the Lord for some time, and Jesus had been patiently bringing them to an understanding of who he was. He began by asking the disciples what others were saying about his identity. There were a variety of answers ranging from John the Baptist to Elijah. But then Jesus shifted his attention to the disciples, asking, "But what about you? Who do you say I am?" Peter, in customary fashion, was quick to respond: "You are the Christ, the Son of the living God" (v. 16).

Peter said a mouthful! From the Jewish perspective there was the expectation of the coming Messiah, the Christ, and Peter's response revealed that he recognized that Jesus was indeed the Anointed One they had been waiting for. Jesus was not like some inanimate idol that the pagans were prone to worship; rather, he was the Son of the *living* God. He was the Source of all life— present, spiritual, and eternal. In every word Peter's response was spoken in the language of a man who was worshipping God with praise and adoration.

The Jews were looking for a Messiah who would come in the splendor and pomp of majestic royalty. Jesus came in unadorned humility. So how did Peter recognize that Jesus was indeed the Son of God and not just a good man, a healer, or a prophet? Jesus confirmed that God the Father had revealed this knowledge to Peter.

Today it is still God who must remove the darkness from our hearts so that we can see the light of Jesus. But when that defining moment comes, we must recognize it and protect it—not rush past it in a frenzy of hurry and worry. And then we must respond, each one of us, when Jesus asks: "But what about you? Who do you say I am?"

Lord Jesus,
I have a feeling that my whole life has been leading
to this question and my answer. At this point I only want
truth. I only have time for truth. Shed light on my heart if
darkness is present, and help me answer out of love and
worship and true recognition that you are the Christ,
the Son of the living God! Amen.

Psalm for the Soul

My soul yearns, even faints,
for the courts of the LORD;
my heart and my flesh cry out
for the living God. (Ps. 84:2)

Great Expectations

*"What do you want me to do for you?" Jesus asked him.
The blind man said, "Rabbi, I want to see."*
MARK 10:51

The man who made this request was Bartimaeus, a blind beggar who routinely sat on the outskirts of the city of Jericho. Most likely he was accustomed to being ignored, shunned, and considered a pest. Because he was blind, he must have trained himself to hear approaching footsteps and to listen to the fragments of the conversations of others.

On this particular day he heard something exciting: Jesus and his disciples were leaving the city with a large crowd surrounding them. In spite of the obstacles of blindness and an uncooperative crowd, Bartimaeus knew that opportunity was knocking as it never had before.

"Jesus, Son of David, have mercy on me!" (v. 47) he cried. This humble Jewish beggar recognized that Jesus was the anticipated Messiah, and he was not about to waste this opportunity by asking for mere bread or alms. This was God—the Creator who *designed* human eyes—he alone would know how to fix them! The beggar's expectations were huge; he wanted a miracle. Jesus did not disappoint him; he rewarded his faith by instantly restoring his sight.

I confess that Bartimaeus's faith shames me. Sometimes when I pray, my expectations are puny or even nonexistent. Recently, however, I had an encounter of my own. Following a series of high-dose chemotherapy treatments, I developed a half-dozen cankerlike sores in my mouth and on my tongue. Although a common side effect of this treatment, they are surprisingly debilitating and affect one's ability to talk, drink, swallow, and even smile. With past treatments I'd had one or two sores that had lasted for several days; I wondered how long this mouthful of sores would linger.

When my phone rang, I considered not answering, but I picked it up and quickly explained the situation to my friend, Karen. She said, "I'm not going to keep you, but let me pray for you." She prayed specifically for my sore mouth, and we hung up.

Almost immediately my mouth began to feel better. In a matter of fifteen or so minutes, all the sores were completely gone! At first I couldn't quite comprehend that my mouth was healed. With past treatments the sores often lingered for several painful days. I was amazed! And then I wondered why I was so astonished to experience answered prayer. God hears every prayer and is capable of answering any and every need. What low expectations of an all-powerful, loving God!

Bartemaeus the beggar asked with great expectations, and the Lord rewarded his faith by opening his eyes to behold his Savior. What a glorious sight after who knows how many years of darkness. Certainly he was dizzy with joy and gratitude. It would have been understandable if he had turned to run and find friends or family, but this formerly blind man suddenly saw things clearly and in love and awe "followed Jesus along the road" (v. 52).

Heavenly Father,
Forgive me for my low expectations of prayer and your
ability and desire to answer. Like Bartemaeus, I want
always to keep in my mind that you are the Son of David,
the Messiah—God! Let me close my eyes in expectant
prayer and open them to see you more clearly.
In your precious name. Amen.

Psalm for the Soul

He upholds the cause of the oppressed
and gives food to the hungry.
The LORD sets prisoners free,
the LORD gives sight to the blind,
the LORD lifts up those who are bowed down,
the LORD loves the righteous. (Ps. 146:7–8)

Twice Blessed

"How can a man be born when he is old?" Nicodemus asked. "Surely he cannot enter a second time into his mother's womb to be born!"
JOHN 3:4

When Billy Graham was in his early eighties, he was asked what had surprised him most about life. He answered, "The brevity of it." Certainly, in the context of eternity, life *is* short. And for those who believe that this life is all there is, the end of it is reason for dread and mourning. But God, in his love and grace, not only blessed us with this brief and precious life; he also blessed us with the opportunity to be born again and spend eternity with him.

When Jesus used the term "born again," a confusion commenced that would reach through the ages. What exactly does it mean to be born again? How on earth can anyone be born again? This kind of birth does not take place on earth at all; it is a *spiritual* birth.

Nicodemus was the first person recorded in the Bible to struggle for understanding, and he went directly to the Source to find out. Nicodemus was not an ignorant man. He was one of the religious elite: a Pharisee and a member of the Jewish ruling counsel. Although he waited until dark to seek out Jesus, he nonetheless approached him with respect: "No one could perform the miraculous signs you are doing if God were not with him" (v. 2). He may have thought Jesus was a prophet or that he possessed some superior religious knowledge.

Jesus ignored these statements and zeroed in on his true need. "No one can see the kingdom of God unless he is born again" (v. 3). It must have jolted Nicodemus to hear such an unusual comment. As a teacher of the Jews, he was accustomed to relying solely on human intelligence and knowledge; he struggled to comprehend how a second physical birth could be accomplished. Without spiritual insight he missed the point.

Although Nicodemus was stuck in a literal mind-set, the Lord led him to the spiritual truth that believing in Jesus is the only way to heaven. "For God so loved the world that he gave his one and only Son, that whoever believes in him shall not perish but have eternal life" (v. 16).

Just as with Nicodemus, God is eager to give us eternal, heavenly life. It awaits all that receive Jesus Christ's sacrificial death on the cross as the price paid for their personal sins. God does not want anyone to stand condemned. In fact, it was for that reason he sent his Son into the world.

Are you born again? Even if you are facing physical death, it's not too late, but after death it will be. Maybe you faithfully attended church all your life or tried your hardest to be a good person. But being a Christian is not a matter of being a good person; it's a matter of being a *new* person. If you are trying to come to belief solely through understanding, you may need to *choose* to believe in order to understand—a small but vital distinction.

Jesus Christ is the Son of God. He died for your sins and wants you to receive the incredible gift of eternal life by believing on him, confessing your sins, and admitting that you need a Savior. You need Jesus. If you haven't done it already, pray the following prayer and receive the gift of eternal life, and you will be born again. You will be twice blessed!

Lord God,
I need you. I have sinned and fallen short of your
perfect standards. Thank you for the incredible sacrifice
of your Son, Jesus, for my sins. I receive him right now
as my Savior and Lord. Thank you for the gift of my
earthly life and the hope of eternal life with you.
In Jesus' holy name. Amen.

Psalm for the Soul

Better is one day in your courts
than a thousand elsewhere;
I would rather be a doorkeeper in the house of my God
than dwell in the tents of the wicked. (Ps. 84:10)

The Promiser Keeps His Promises

Promises are easy to make. However, we all know that the pathway of life is damp with the tears caused by broken promises. Even marriage, our most cherished ceremony of promise, has become a primary arena of broken vows, shattering homes and hearts. Then there are the disappointments caused by implied promises, false claims, and outright deception, and it is easy to see why we have become skeptical. "If it sounds too good to be true, it probably is" has become the catchphrase of a savvy generation. We eventually learn that a promise is only as meaningful as the capability and integrity of the one who makes the promise.

God's promises cannot be separated from God's character. When we look into the essence of the promise, we learn about the nature of the Promiser. For instance, if we are experiencing fear, we might turn to Luke 12:6–7: "Are not five sparrows sold for two pennies? Yet not one of them is forgotten by God. Indeed, the very hairs of your head are all numbered. Don't be afraid; you are worth more than many sparrows." At first this may seem like a simple reassurance that God cares about us. But when we look deeper, we find we can learn some valuable truths about God. Who but an all-knowing, everywhere-present God could keep track of the untold millions of humble sparrows? Who but a God of love would *care* how many hairs populate your head? Who but a God of mercy would tenderly note the death of a sparrow or care that our unspoken fears are robbing us of peace and confidence in God's love? Looking at Scripture in the light of the majesty of God enables us to lay hold of truth and the knowledge and character of God.

Isn't it astounding to realize that the God of the universe desires to have a relationship with you and reveal himself to you?

Therefore, as you ponder these promises and Scriptures of hope, remember the character and power of the Most High God who made them. This is by no means a comprehensive list of promises. My hope is that as you feed on his Word, you will contemplate our Savior and seek to know the Promiser much more than the promise.

ANGER

(Remember: God is just.)

> A gentle answer turns away wrath,
> but a harsh word stirs up anger. (Prov. 15:1)

> "In your anger do not sin": Do not let the sun go down while you are still angry. (Eph. 4:26)

> Get rid of all bitterness, rage and anger, brawling and slander, along with every form of malice. Be kind and compassionate to one another, forgiving each other, just as in Christ God forgave you. (Eph. 4:31–32)

> Do not take revenge, my friends, but leave room for God's wrath, for it is written: "It is mine to avenge; I will repay," says the LORD. (Rom. 12:19)

COMFORT

(Remember: God's power is limitless.)

> God is our refuge and strength,
> an ever-present help in trouble.
> Therefore we will not fear, though the earth give way
> and the mountains fall into the heart of the sea,
> though its waters roar and foam
> and the mountains quake with their surging.
> (Ps. 46:1–3)

> Though I walk in the midst of trouble,
> you preserve my life;
> you stretch out your hand against the anger of my foes,
> with your right hand you save me. (Ps. 138:7)

> "I have told you these things, so that in me you may have peace. In this world you will have trouble. But take heart! I have overcome the world." (John 16:33)

For just as the sufferings of Christ flow over into our lives, so also through Christ our comfort overflows. (2 Cor. 1:5)

ETERNAL LIFE

(Remember: Through Jesus Christ we have eternal life.)

Jesus said to her, "I am the resurrection and the life. He who believes in me will live, even though he dies; and whoever lives and believes in me will never die. Do you believe this?" (John 11:25–26)

So will it be with the resurrection of the dead. The body that is sown is perishable, it is raised imperishable; it is sown in dishonor, it is raised in glory; it is sown in weakness, it is raised in power; it is sown a natural body, it is raised a spiritual body. (1 Cor. 15:42–44)

"He will wipe every tear from their eyes. There will be no more death or mourning or crying or pain, for the old order of things has passed away." (Rev. 21:4)

For the wages of sin is death, but the gift of God is eternal life in Christ Jesus our Lord. (Rom. 6:23)

FACING DEATH

(Remember: God has conquered death.)

"Where, O death, is your victory? Where, O death, is your sting?" The sting of death is sin, and the power of sin is the law. But thanks be to God! He gives us the victory through our Lord Jesus Christ. (1 Cor. 15:55–57)

Brothers, we do not want you to be ignorant about those who fall asleep, or to grieve like the rest of men, who have no hope. We believe that Jesus died and rose again and so we believe that God will bring with Jesus those who have fallen asleep in him. (1 Thess. 4:13–14)

We are confident, I say, and would prefer to be away from the body and at home with the Lord. So we make it our goal to please him, whether we are at home in the body or away from it. (2 Cor. 5:8–9)

Since the children have flesh and blood, he too shared in their humanity so that by his death he might destroy him who holds the power of death—that is, the

devil—and free those who all their lives were held in
slavery by their fear of death. (Heb. 2:14–15)

FEAR

(Remember: The Lord is present everywhere.)
    He will cover you with his feathers,
    and under his wings you will find refuge;
    his faithfulness will be your shield and rampart.
    You will not fear the terror of night,
    nor the arrow that flies by day,
    nor the pestilence that stalks in the darkness,
    nor the plague that destroys at midday. (Ps. 91:4–6)

    The LORD is my light and my salvation—
    whom shall I fear?
    The LORD is the stronghold of my life—
    of whom shall I be afraid? . . .
    Though an army besiege me,
    my heart will not fear;
    though war break out against me,
    even then will I be confident. (Ps. 27:1, 3)

    No, in all these things we are more than conquerors
through him who loved us. For I am convinced that neither death nor life, neither angels nor demons, neither
the present nor the future, nor any powers, neither
height nor depth, nor anything else in all creation, will
be able to separate us from the love of God that is in
Christ Jesus our LORD. (Rom. 8:37–39)

    So we say with confidence, "The Lord is my helper;
I will not be afraid. What can man do to me?"
(Heb. 13:6)

FORGIVENESS

(Remember: God is a God of grace.)
    "I will put my law in their minds
    and write it on their hearts.
    I will be their God,
    and they will be my people. . . .
    For I will forgive their wickedness
    and will remember their sins no more."
    (Jer. 31:33–34)

For he has rescued us from the dominion of darkness and brought us into the kingdom of the Son he loves, in whom we have redemption, the forgiveness of sins. (Col. 1:13–14)

If we confess our sins, he is faithful and just and will forgive us our sins and purify us from all unrighteousness. (1 John 1:9)

In him we have redemption through his blood, the forgiveness of sins, in accordance with the riches of God's grace that he lavished on us with all wisdom and understanding. (Eph. 1:7–8)

GUIDANCE

(Remember: God is all-knowing.)

"For I know the plans I have for you," declares the LORD, "plans to prosper you and not to harm you, plans to give you hope and a future. Then you will call upon me and come and pray to me, and I will listen to you." (Jer. 29:11–12)

Whether you turn to the right or to the left, your ears will hear a voice behind you saying, "This is the way; walk in it." (Isa. 30:21)

In his heart a man plans his course,
but the LORD determines his steps. (Prov. 16:9)

For this God is our God for ever and ever;
he will be our guide even to the end. (Ps. 48:14)

HEAVEN

(Remember: God is the Creator.)

But in keeping with his promise we are looking forward to a new heaven and a new earth, the home of righteousness. (2 Pet. 3:13)

"You alone are the LORD. You made the heavens, even the highest heavens, and all their starry host, the earth and all that is on it, the seas and all that is in them. You give life to everything, and the multitudes of heaven worship you." (Neh. 9:6–7)

For here we do not have an enduring city, but we are looking for the city that is to come. (Heb. 13:14)

And there were loud voices in heaven, which said: "The kingdom of the world has become the kingdom of our Lord and of his Christ, and he will reign for ever and ever." (Rev. 11:15)

HELP IN TROUBLES

(Remember: God is above all.)

You are my hiding place;
you will protect me from trouble
and surround me with songs of deliverance.
(Ps. 32:7)

Then no harm will befall you,
no disaster will come near your tent.
For he will command his angels concerning you
to guard you in all your ways. (Ps. 91:10–11)

"I have told you these things, so that in me you may have peace. In this world you will have trouble. But take heart! I have overcome the world." (John 16:33)

"When you pass through the waters,
I will be with you;
and when you pass through the rivers,
they will not sweep over you.
When you walk through the fire,
you will not be burned;
the flames will not set you ablaze.
For I am the LORD, your God,
the Holy One of Israel, your Savior." (Isa. 43:2–3)

HOPE

(Remember: God is good.)

When calamity comes, the wicked are brought down,
but even in death the righteous have a refuge.
(Prov. 14:32)

Praise be to the God and Father of our Lord Jesus Christ! In his great mercy he has given us new birth into a living hope through the resurrection of Jesus Christ from the dead. (1 Pet. 1:3)

May the God of hope fill you with all joy and peace
as you trust in him, so that you may overflow with hope
by the power of the Holy Spirit. (Rom. 15:13)

I pray also that the eyes of your heart may be
enlightened in order that you may know the hope to
which he has called you, the riches of his glorious inheritance in the saints, and his incomparably great power
for us who believe. (Eph. 1:18–19)

JOY

(Remember: God is holy.)
Light is shed upon the righteous
and joy on the upright in heart.
Rejoice in the LORD, you who are righteous,
and praise his holy name. (Ps. 97:11–12)

In him our hearts rejoice, for we trust in his holy
name. (Ps. 33:21)

But you will rejoice in the LORD
and glory in the Holy One of Israel. (Isa. 41:16)

For the kingdom of God is not a matter of eating and
drinking, but of righteousness, peace and joy in the Holy
Spirit. (Rom. 14:17)

LONELINESS

(Remember: God is merciful.)
Yet I am poor and needy;
may the Lord think of me.
You are my help and my deliverer;
O my God, do not delay. (Ps. 40:17)

Then you will call, and the LORD will answer;
you will cry for help, and he will say: Here am I.
(Isa. 58:9)

"I will be a Father to you
and you will be my sons and daughters,
says the Lord Almighty.' (2 Cor. 6:18)

The LORD is a refuge for the oppressed,
a stronghold in times of trouble. (Ps. 9:9)

PEACE

(Remember: God is faithful.)

Peace I leave with you; my peace I give you. I do not give to you as the world gives. Do not let your hearts be troubled and do not be afraid. (John 14:27)

Let us hold unswervingly to the hope we profess, for he who promised is faithful. (Heb. 10:23)

So we say with confidence, "The Lord is my helper; I will not be afraid. What can man do to me?" (Heb. 13:6)

Those who know your name will trust in you,
for you, LORD, have never forsaken those who seek you. (Ps. 9:10)

"Though the mountains be shaken
and the hills be removed,
yet my unfailing love for you will not be shaken
nor my covenant of peace be removed,"
says the LORD, who has compassion on you.
(Isa. 54:10)

PATIENCE/PERSEVERANCE

(Remember: God is wise.)

Then you will understand the fear of the LORD
and find the knowledge of God.
For the LORD gives wisdom,
and from his mouth come knowledge and understanding.
He holds victory in store for the upright,
he is a shield to those whose walk is blameless.
(Prov. 2:5–7)

We do not want you to become lazy, but to imitate those who through faith and patience inherit what has been promised. (Heb. 6:12)

You need to persevere so that when you have done the will of God, you will receive what he has promised. (Heb. 10:36)

Consider it pure joy, my brothers, whenever you face trials of many kinds, because you know that the testing

of your faith develops perseverance. Perseverance must
finish its work so that you may be mature and complete,
not lacking anything. (James 1:2–4)

PRAYER

(Remember: God listens and answers.)

"Ask and it will be given to you; seek and you will
find; knock and the door will be opened to you. For
everyone who asks receives; he who seeks finds; and to
him who knocks, the door will be opened."
(Matt. 7:7–8)

This is the confidence we have in approaching God:
that if we ask anything according to his will, he hears
us. And if we know that he hears us—whatever we
ask—we know that we have what we asked of him.
(1 John 5:14–15)

Before they call I will answer;
while they are still speaking I will hear. (Isa. 65:24)

Therefore confess your sins to each other and pray
for each other so that you may be healed. The prayer of
a righteous man is powerful and effective. (James 5:16)

SALVATION

(Remember: God is love.)

For God so loved the world that he gave his one and
only Son, that whoever believes in him shall not perish
but have eternal life. (John 3:16)

The LORD appeared to us in the past saying:
"I have loved you with an everlasting love;
I have drawn you with loving-kindness." (Jer. 31:3)

This is love: not that we loved God, but that he loved
us and sent his Son as an atoning sacrifice for our sins.
(1 John 4:10)

But when the kindness and love of God our Savior
appeared, he saved us, not because of righteous things
we had done, but because of his mercy. He saved us
through the washing of rebirth and renewal by the Holy
Spirit, whom he poured out on us generously through
Jesus Christ our Savior. (Titus 3:4–6)

SICKNESS/HEALING

(Remember: God is sovereign.)

Is any one of you sick? He should call the elders of the church to pray over him and anoint him with oil in the name of the Lord. And the prayer offered in faith will make the sick person well, the Lord will raise him up. If he has sinned, he will be forgiven. Therefore confess your sins to each other and pray for each other so that you may be healed. The prayer of a righteous man is powerful and effective. (James 5:14–16)

> Heal me, O LORD, and I will be healed;
> save me and I will be saved,
> for you are the one I praise. (Jer. 17:14)

"But so that you may know that the Son of Man has authority on earth to forgive sins. . . ." Then he said to the paralytic, "Get up, take your mat and go home."
And the man got up and went home. (Matt. 9:6–7)

"Do not be afraid, for I am with you." (Isa. 43:5)

SORROW

(Remember: God is compassionate.)

> Blessed are those who mourn,
> for they will be comforted. (Matt. 5:4)

He will wipe every tear from their eyes. There will be no more death or mourning or crying or pain, for the old order of things has passed away. (Rev. 21:4)

> The ransomed of the LORD will return.
> They will enter Zion with singing;
> everlasting joy will crown their heads.
> Gladness and joy will overtake them,
> and sorrow and sighing will flee away. (Isa. 51:11)

"You will grieve, but your grief will turn to joy. A woman giving birth to a child has pain because her time has come; but when her baby is born she forgets the anguish because of her joy that a child is born into the world. So with you: Now is your time of grief, but I will see you again and you will rejoice, and no one will take away your joy." (John 16:20–22)

STRENGTH

(Remember: God is powerful.)

But those who hope in the LORD
will renew their strength.
They will soar on wings like eagles;
they will run and not grow weary,
they will walk and not be faint. (Isa. 40:31)

But he said to me, "My grace is sufficient for you,
for my power is made perfect in weakness. Therefore
I will boast all the more gladly about my weaknesses,
so that Christ's power may rest on me." (2 Cor. 12:9)

And we pray this in order that you may live a life worthy of the Lord and may please him in every way: bearing fruit in every good work, growing in the knowledge of God, being strengthened with all power according to his glorious might so that you may have great endurance and patience, and joyfully giving thanks to the Father, who has qualified you to share in the inheritance of the saints in the kingdom of light. (Col. 1:10–12)

I can do everything through him who gives me strength. (Phil. 4:13)

WORSHIP

(Remember: Our God is the Most High God.)

All the earth bows down to you;
they sing praise to you,
they sing praise to your name. (Ps. 66:4)

Ascribe to the LORD the glory due his name;
bring an offering and come into his courts.
Worship the LORD in the splendor of his holiness;
tremble before him, all the earth. (Ps. 96:8–9)

Therefore, since we are receiving a kingdom that cannot be shaken, let us be thankful, and so worship God acceptably with reverence and awe, for our "God is a consuming fire." (Heb. 12:28–29)

Thomas said to him, "My Lord and my God!" (John 20:28)

Remember: God keeps his promises!

Prayer to Receive Christ as Your Savior

Lord Jesus,

I need you. I am a sinner and I ask for your forgiveness of my sins. I want to turn away from my sins and turn toward you in faith. I believe that you died for me on the cross and then you rose from the grave. Please come into my life and my heart. I want to follow you for the rest of my life and spend eternity with you. Thank you for loving me, paying for my sins, and preparing a place for me in heaven.

In Jesus' name. Amen.